Christian Poetry in Canada

✝Christian Poetry in Canada

EDITED BY DAVID A. KENT

ECW PRESS

CANADIAN CATALOGUING IN PUBLICATION DATA

Main entry under title:
Christian poetry in Canada

Includes index.
ISBN 1-55022-015-2

1. Christian poetry, Canadian (English).* 2. Canadian poetry (English)
– 19th century.* 3. Canadian poetry (English) – 20th century.*
I. Kent, David A., 1948– .

PS8287.C35C35 1989 C811'.088'0382 C88-094267-3
PR9195.85.C35C35 1989

The cover features details of a watercolour by Jane Watanabe.

Design and imaging by ECW Production Services, Sydenham, Ontario.

Distributed by University of Toronto Press, 5201 Dufferin Street,
North York, Ontario M3H 5T8

Published by ECW PRESS, 307 Coxwell Avenue, Toronto, Ontario
M4L 3B5

ACKNOWLEDGEMENTS

"Easter," "A Story," "Person," and " . . . Person, or A Hymn on and to the Holy Ghost" by Margaret Avison. Used by permission of the Canadian Publishers, McClelland and Stewart, Toronto.

"Water and Worship: an open air service on the Gatineau River," "The Bible to be Believed," "Listening," "Oughtiness Ousted," and "We the Poor who are Always with us" are reprinted from *sunblue* by Margaret Avison with the permission of Lancelot Press.

"O, None of That," "All You Need Is a Screw-Driver!" and "Known" are used with the permission of Margaret Avison.

Poems by Alfred Bailey are reprinted by permission of the author.

Poems by Robert Beum are reprinted by permission of the author.

"Good Friday Performances," "Easter Sunday, Quaker Meeting," and "You Say" by Elizabeth Brewster are reprinted with the permission of Oberon Press. "Supposition," "Poem to the Blessed Virgin," and "Poem for the Year of Faith" are used with the permission of Elizabeth Brewster.

Poems by J.M. Cameron are reprinted by the permission of the author.

Poems by Wanda Campbell are used with the permission of the author.

Poems by Anne Corkett are used with the permission of the author.

Poems by Fred Cogswell are used with the permission of the author.

Poems by Theodore Colson are used with the permission of the author.

Poems by David Creelman are used with the permission of the author.

Poems by Roy Daniells from *The Chequered Shade*. Used by permission of the Canadian Publishers, McClelland and Stewart, Toronto.

Poems by Barry Dempster are used with the permission of the author.

"Such Lovely" by John Ditsky is reprinted by permission of Ontario Review Press. "On Good Friday," "Voyeur," and "September Evening Bicycle Ride" by John Ditsky are reprinted by permission of Vesta Publications.

"Has and Is" and "Nor Any Other Creature" by Robert Finch are reprinted with thanks to the author and The Porcupine's Quill, Inc., Publishers. Other poems by Robert Finch are used with the permission of the author.

Poems by Gail Fox are used with the permission of the author.

Poems by Timothy Gibbon are used with the permission of the author.

Poems by Robert Gibbs are used with the permission of the author.

Poems by Glenn Hayes are used with the permission of the author.

Poems by Maggie Helwig are used with the permission of the author.

Poems by George Johnston are used with the permission of the author.

Poems by Leo Kennedy are used with the permission of the author.

"The Returning" by Watson Kirkconnell is reprinted with the permission of Janet Kirkconnell.

Poems by M. Travis Lane are used with the permission of the author.

Poems by Kenneth Leslie are used with the permission of Rosaleen Leslie Dickson.

Poems by Tim Lilburn are used with the permission of the author.

Poems by Douglas Lochhead are used with the permission of the author.

Poems by Louis Mackay are used with the permission of Pierre Mackay.

"The Innocents," "The Natural Mother," and "The Fisherman" from *Poems Twice Told* by Jay Macpherson, © Oxford University Press Canada 1981; used by permission of the publisher.

Poems by R.J. MacSween are used with the permission of the author.

"John of the Cross II (Cautery)" from *Conversing with Paradise* (1986) by Susan McCaslin is reprinted by permission of Golden Eagle Press. "The Beauty of the Law," "He Could Not Be Hid," and "The Pattern of the City" are used with the permission of Susan McCaslin.

"Vocations" from *Man in Love* (1985) by Richard Outram is reprinted by permission of The Porcupine's Quill, Inc. "Bittersweet," "Young Man Enmeshed," "Infant," and "Other" are used with the permission of Richard Outram.

Poems by Michael Parr are used with the permission of the author.

Poems by E.J. Pratt are reprinted by permission of University of Toronto Press.

"Andrew Whittaker, Local Preacher" from *Ashbourn* (1986) by John Reibetanz is reprinted with the permission of Véhicule Press. Other poems by John Reibetanz are used with the permission of the author.

"On the Supernatural" and "Martyrs" from *Shapes and Sounds* (1968) by W.W.E. Ross are reprinted by permission of Harcourt, Brace, Jovanovich. "The Stream of Life" and "On Angels" by W.W.E. Ross are used with the permission of Mrs. Mary Hutton.

Poems by F.R. Scott are from his *Collected Poems* and are used by permission of the Canadian Publishers, McClelland and Stewart, Toronto.

"Calvary" from *A Classic Shade* by A.J.M. Smith is used by permission of the Canadian Publishers, McClelland and Stewart, Toronto. "The Bird," "Good Friday," and "Beside One Dead" are published with the permission of William Toye for the Estate of A.J.M. Smith.

Poems by Kay Smith are used with the permission of the author.

Poems by Colleen Thibaudeau are used with the permission of the author.

Poems by Margo Swiss are used with the permission of the author.

"Canticle of Darkness" from *Friday's Child* by Wilfred Watson is reprinted by permission of the author. "There is no penance due to innocence/deconstructed" from *Poems* (Longspoon/NeWest, 1986) was first published in *Mass on Cowback* (Longspoon, 1982) and is used by permission of Wilfred Watson.

Poems by George Whalley are reprinted by permission of Mrs. Elizabeth Whalley.

Poems by James Wreford are used with the permission of the author.

for Jonathan

TABLE OF CONTENTS

INTRODUCTION

In his conclusion to the first edition of the *Literary History of Canada*, Northrop Frye makes the following statement: "Religion has been a major — perhaps the major — cultural force in Canada, at least down to the last generation or two." In some respects, religion continues to be a hidden, often unacknowledged reality in Canadian culture. As McLuhan observed of the information environment, the presence of something so much a part of our immediate (or recent) lives frequently remains invisible to our perception precisely because it is so familiar or pervasive.[1]

So it may not be surprising to observe the comparative lack of attention paid to religious poetry by Canadian academics, literary critics and editors, and other students of this country's literature. Especially during the explosive proliferation of the last two decades, countless anthologies of poetry have been published. Their subjects have ranged from the æsthetic avant-garde (concrete and sound poetry) to poetry by women and by "minority" groups, including native people and various ethnic communities (Blacks, Japanese-Canadians, Italian-Canadians, and so on); and from new "waves" of young poets to poets identified with various regions of the country (British Columbia, the Prairies, Quebec, Atlantic Canada, and Newfoundland). There have even been collections featuring Mennonite and Jewish writers. Why, then, in all this time and during this surge of literary activity, has there been published only one modest, and rather narrowly defined, anthology of Christian poetry — that edited by Harry Houton for Wedge Publications in 1971?

The question is not easy to answer. Religious faith, of course, has seldom been fashionable. Certainly it has not been fashionable during the successive phases of idealistic rebellion against authority and of materialistic self-indulgence that have characterized so much of Canadian cultural life since the 1960s, when Canadian literature effectively emerged as a subject for intensive study. Moreover, in the academic world, where so much of our literary culture seems to be contained and manufactured, not only has religion become intellectually unrespectable (Marxism, structuralism, post-structuralism, or deconstruction all apparently being more desirable "theoretical" or critical stances to be identified with[2]), but the institutional substructures — the religious colleges of the last generation, for example —

have at the same time been steadily diminishing in status and influence. Their secular surrogates have first principles about the world and experience that are radically different. And secularism has little interest in those religious values or modes of expression from which it has so successfully sought to divorce itself. In public schools, too, the increasing tendency has been to withdraw elements of Christian tradition from the classroom in order to avoid possible insults to the values of minority cultures.

Furthermore, among poets as well as academics, Christian poetry is all too often perceived as being almost entirely in the Helen Steiner Rice vein: overflowing with clichés, sentimentality, tiring platitudes, and boring exhortations. Its range of thought is assumed to be narrow and confined because of its informing "ideology," as if Christianity — viewed dispassionately from a certain intellectual height — were simply another system of philosophical concepts, and naïve and untenable ones at that. One apparent result is that most critics prefer and praise poetry of existential struggle in which the artist-hero battles for self-realization or against the evils of a repressive society (religion being portrayed as an agency of repression). In the process, the artist may disclose the "inherent" disorder and insurmountable contradictions of existence and then repudiate traditional analyses of experience. (The alarming number of suicides among twentieth-century writers is, in part, testimony to a widespread rejection of religious solace.) This inclination, in both poetry and its criticism, contrasts the artist-hero with the supposed complacency of individuals with a religious faith, as if the commitment to that faith involved a halt to self-development or personal growth. Such views are themselves encumbered with ideological baggage marked with the label, "Romantic ideals of artist." For the Romantic critic and artist of a century and a half ago, in rebellion against an *ancien régime* of neoclassical aesthetic values, the creative genius of the artist was autonomous. In turn, the creative act was conceived in analogy to God's creativity, in effect bringing something into being *ex nihilo*, while the product of this possession was itself supposedly outside time and circumstance and uncontaminated with intentionality. The legacy of these Romantic notions buried in "modern" attitudes is only beginning to be recognized.

The premises and values of Christian art are very different from the ruling orthodoxy. Christian art cannot be, finally, an art of pessimism or despair but rather one of hope — not the pious optimism of a debased evangelism, but the hard-won commitment to life secured through the gracious dynamics of faith. Also, at the heart of religious faith is an acknowledgement of mystery fundamentally intolerable to intellect. When articulated, mystery is expressed in paradox and symbol, the language of poetry. The Christian poet is more likely to subordinate consciously his own individuality and creativity to the will of God. He would not claim to be inventing or discovering truth; rather he is the student of God's purposes, patiently learning about the providential will and seeking, through his craft, to disclose that reality to others. His art is therefore riddled not so much with didacticism as with intentionality, explicit or implicit. His art of words becomes an offering to the Word, and his gesture can take a wide variety of forms: celebration and praise, petition, confession, the liturgy or "work" of witness and testimony, exegesis or commentary on scripture, the dramatizing of an experience of alienation and reconcilation, exhortation, homily, and so on. Religious faith does not simplify poetry: it can complicate it enormously, as any study of the most sophisticated religious poetry testifies.

And yet, despite all the potential for formal and attitudinal variety, the Christian poet faces certain perennial problems. A central difficulty is one that springs out of our Romantic inheritance and one which W. H. Auden acknowledges in his well-known essay, "Postscript: Christianity and Art." Thinking especially about the confessional poems of Donne and Hopkins, Auden wondered aloud: "Is there not something a little odd, to say the least, about making an admirable public object out of one's feelings of guilt and penitence before God?"[3] The self-display involved in writing lyrics was for a long time an impediment to religious poetry, even to the writing and singing of hymns. In the middle of the nineteenth century, for example, Isaac Disraeli could still make the following comments about the distasteful practice of insinuating hymn singing into church services and thereby displacing the traditional singing of psalms: "It has not, perhaps, been remarked that psalm-singing, or metrical psalms, degenerated into those scandalous compositions which, under the abused title of *hymns*, are now used by some sects."[4] Ironically, the legitimizing of self-expression in the modern period was a gradual development generated by Romanticism. Nevertheless, this matter remains one with which the Christian poet such as Auden, evidently shy of solipsism, continues to struggle.

To meet this kind of difficulty in his vocation, the Christian poet must be rigorously self-conscious. He may have to overcome both a puritanical attitude towards art prevalent in some branches of Christianity as well as elements of "Anti-intellectualism in the faith community," as Tim Lilburn puts it in a recent article.[5] After all, the gradual division between sacred and secular art over the course of the past several centuries should not obscure the fact that religion and art, in their natural antipathy to materialism and mass culture, are important allies amid rampant secularism. It would be possible to try to describe aspects of a Christian poetic by referring to issues of style (and cite the complex simplicity of George Herbert's lyrics as an example), to the matter of inspiration (and stress grace, not genius, or the Holy Spirit, rather than the Muse, as the source), or to the question of the poet's relationship to nature and society. But to do so would require a book. One recent study does attest to the genuine complexity of these larger questions confronting the Christian poet. In *Towards a Christian Poetics*, Michael Edwards writes of the fundamental paradox at the heart of the Christian writer's role and dilemma. "Writing really does re-create the world for us, but is only a sign, an analogy, of Re-creation proper, which is in the power of God. . . . To write is to succeed and fail, to remain in an unresolved dialectical process. . . . [The writer] attempts to re-create the world through words, as God created the world and will re-create it through the Word; he fails to do so — his work being neither a scripture nor the text of the world to come — because of his alienation from that Word, because at the end of the day, at the end of the re-creative process, his text is still written in a fallen language."[6] If Christianity is a religion of paradoxes like these, there is little wonder the Christian writer cannot avoid becoming entangled in the fundamental issues of his craft, such as the very texture of the language he employs. That he attempts to write at all must suggest that, together with St. Augustine so many centuries ago, he believes in the final efficacy of language: i.e., the necessity for, and utility of, language in spite of its inadequacies. Marcia Colish has concisely summarized Augustine's understanding of this issue, and her description is worth quoting for its continuing relevance to Christian writing: "Once joined to God in Christ, human nature is restored in mind and body, and man's faculty of speech is empowered to carry on the work of Incarnation in expressing the Word to the world. For Augustine, redeemed speech becomes a mirror through which men may know God in this life by faith. And Christian eloquence becomes, both literally and figuratively, a vessel of the Spirit, bearing the Word to mankind, incorporating men into the new covenant of Christ and preparing them through its mediation for the face-to-face knowledge of God in the beatific vision."[7] This idea of redeemed language makes Christian poetry possible, and means that, at its best, such poetry may itself be a species of Christian eloquence.

In the present anthology — which is concerned entirely with the poetry of English Canada — my aim has been to compile a selection of Christian poetry by English Canadian poets which would include (1) poetry that is in some sense representative; (2) poetry that is excellent in its own right; and (3) poetry that will demonstrate the formal variety possible in this genre. Although I might easily have started the anthology with Robert Hayman's *Quodlibets* from the early seventeenth century, his work is so temporally isolated from what eventually follows it that to include samples would be to follow chronology too slavishly. I have therefore passed over the seventeenth and eighteenth centuries and have begun the selections with Susanna Moodie in the nineteenth century. Only then did Canada really begin to emerge as a distinct society. Visitors began to stay permanently, and a cultural life was gradually born. I was also tempted at one time to include extracts of Henry Alline's *Hymns and Spiritual Songs* from the eighteenth century. However, unlike Donald Davie in his *New Oxford Book of Christian Verse*,[8] I have followed the view that hymns are not poetry because they elevate melody and musical rhythms above language; the words become accompaniment and embellishment rather than possessing their own integrity and authenticity. Similarly, I have not included the work of early clergymen such as Joseph Clinch (*The Captivity of Babylon and Other Poems*, 1840), Joshua Marsden (from his *Leisure Hours*, 1812, or the later *Poems on Methodism*, 1848), or Bishop Mountain (*Songs of the Wilderness*, 1846) because, as in the case of hymns, these writers' skills with language have been subordinated to other concerns.

Of course, any anthology is the result of considerable rummaging about; the undertaking has also meant examining a great deal of transient work of poor quality and choosing what will adequately reflect that large mass of forgotten material. In such matters, one often acts on instinct and faith and hopes the results will be acceptable. I have, understandably, sought to select poetry written by Christians, although I can hardly say that any test was administered to the contributors. The fact remains, I believe, that the faith of the writer is not the final criterion for inclusion in this anthology. What is central is the text of the poem. A poem that explicitly enunciates, or that just suggests, Christian perspectives on experience can be efficacious independent of the author's state of mind. Indeed, I have tried to include poems that express those less than pious, but genuine and important, emotions like anxiety, doubt, anger, and despair — feelings that are an integral part of our human and religious experience. Religious faith is no life insurance policy that guarantees our escape from suffering in its manifold forms, but it does help us to handle the crises represented by these reactions to common experiences of loss and disappointment. One final observation: my intention in adhering to the criterion of explicitly Christian poems was partly an attempt to avoid vaguely spiritualist poetry (with some kind of transcendental yearnings) that seems to pass as "religious poetry" in some quarters.

Like the rest of nineteenth-century Canadian poetry, the earlier Christian poems I have included in this selection bear obvious marks of their English models, not only in formal ways but also in matters of theme, tone, and posture. Duncan Campbell Scott's "Meditation at Perugia," for example, mentions the science versus religion debate that preoccupied Victorians; his sentimental attachment to things Medieval (voiced in Tennysonian accents) also helps to date this poem. Marjorie Pickthall's "Père Lalemant" at least, we might say, Canadianizes this admiration for saints by canonizing a Jesuit priest of the seventeenth century. Present in this body of work, too, are the familiar Christian paradoxes. Mrs. Yule plays with the inversions of "living" and "dying" wittily in her poem of this title. Mrs. Leprohon dwells on the Christmas scene in conventional ways, and the pilgrimage motif is strong in almost all of the Victorian writers, as Sangster's "My Prayer" and Dewart's marching song, "Lead Thou Me On," illustrate. There is also the theme of the prodigal son, the Christian everyman who has fallen away from God into sin but who returns to seek forgiveness; this theme informs both John Reade's work as well as Pauline Johnson's "A Prodigal."

On the whole, there is a reluctance among the early writers to allow themselves much overt self-expression. Although this inhibition is perhaps characteristic of some religious poetry, it is — as I noted above — also a characteristic of Victorian culture. It is particularly strong in the poetry of the first half of the century before the tide of the Romantic worship of self invaded the arts. For writers like Moodie, Reade, and McPherson, religion transcends everything worldly, offering the faithful refuge, relief, peace. McLachlan's "Old Hannah," for example, resembles a Wordsworthian solitary whose suffering has given her strength to overcome external circumstance. Many of the speakers in poems from this period seem to aspire to the same state of quietus. Lyricism, because self-centred, is considered close to idolatry and thus impiety. These poets often wrote paraphrases of the Psalms (as in the example by Susanna Moodie), thereby adhering as closely as possible to the authority of the Inspired Word of God. In a similar way, some poets sought to dramatize Biblical passages or stories (John McPherson's "Probation" is an extrapolation from one Scriptural passage). The use of a Biblical epigraph, moreover, was a way of signalling the priority of the sacred text over the poem (its commentary), as well as of sending the reader back to the true source of religious truth. The omnipresence of death in everyday life explains both its stubborn presence in the poetry as well as the other-worldly ambience of many of the poems. The Neoplatonic qualities of John McPherson's "Earthly Joy" (where the "upper sphere" is pure) are equally evident in Isabella Valancy

Crawford's "His Clay," and the implied *contemptus mundi* attitude is a natural corollary to them.

There are important transformations in the religious lyric as we follow it from the second half of the nineteenth century into the twentieth century, changes which naturally mirror those occurring in secular verse of the same period. The first recognizably modern voice among the nineteenth century poets is Sir Charles G. D. Roberts. His personal lyricism as well as his unashamed celebration of visionary, even mystical, experience mark him as a genuine heir of the English Romantics. The natural images of an earlier poet, such as Mary Herbert, function as emblems of God's power but not as felt evidence of His presence in the world (as in, for example, Roberts's "An Evening Communion," not included here). A similar combination of mystical transport and affirmation of immanence is seen in Lampman's "New Year's Eve"; moreover, the boldness of the "I" in many poems by Lampman looks ahead to the even greater freedom enjoyed by twentieth-century poets.

The wide range of twentieth-century Christian poetry in Canada is directly proportionate to the generally experimental and rebellious spirit of modern artists in reacting to their Victorian forebears. All areas of life — politics, social life, sexuality — have become available for treatment in the increasingly forthright work of modern poets. Christian poetry also changed dramatically; the very diversity of modern voices represented in this collection indicates how difficult it is to make useful generalizations regarding this body of work. Christian poetry can be brutally honest as well as reserved; it can be coy and witty, like Roy Daniells's sonnets; celebrative or sardonic, as in M. Travis Lane's poems; angry and indignant (see, for example, Louis Mackay's "Sonnet for 1938" for some memorable parodic satire). The poems of Elizabeth Brewster included here vary from the strongly devotional "Poem to the Blessed Virgin" to a confession of sexual fantasy interfering with prayer in "Easter Sunday, Quaker Meeting." Poets may display their formal skills in sonnets (Robert Finch) and sestinas (Robert Gibbs), or their desire for freedom in open, sometimes idiosyncratic forms, including the dramatic monologue (John Reibetanz, Margo Swiss), or in a bare, plain-speaking story (Margaret Avison's "A Story"). Craft and order can be used to control powerful emotion (as we sense in George Johnston) or to describe ecstatic experience (Gail Fox's "Prayer Meeting"). As Avison has said in an essay on writing Christian poetry, "No subject matter is ruled out. . . . "[9] With prohibitions relaxed, poets can speak of the tortures of lust (Richard Outram's "Young Man Enmeshed"), of the struggle of faith with doubt, of the afterlife (Anne Corkett's "Temporal Zone"), of social concerns (Timmy Gibbon), of organized religion, and of television evangelists (Barry Dempster). And these subjects can be handled in distinctive ways, from the compact style of A. J. M. Smith and the cerebral manner of J. M. Cameron to the lucid minimalism of Robert Beum or energetic urgency of Tim Lilburn. Quite simply, the achievement of Canadian Christian poetry is impressive. The work included here should demonstrate that the tradition of religious expression through poetry in Canada has been a vigorous one and that it does indeed continue.

There are many acknowledgements I am happy to offer. I am, first of all, grateful to Jay Johnson, Michael Darling, and the late George Wicken who, as office mates in the English graduate programme at York University a decade ago now, thought the idea for this kind of anthology had some merit when I first mentioned it. Margaret Avison gave me important early encouragement to proceed and offered a number of practical suggestions to get matters going. Various editors gave me suggestions at one time or another which I much appreciated: George Woodcock, George Sanderson, and Michael Higgins, with my special thanks to Robert Gibbs and Dean Peerman for their very helpful assistance. I also wish to thank Fr. Robert Ross and, once again, Michael Darling for reading through the manuscript and suggesting very useful revisions. Miss Ronwen Stock's long-standing interest in my progress kept the idea alive over a number of years, and Sister Carol Lindholm's repeated affirmations have been a source of considerable strength. I am indebted, once more, to Jack David for taking this project on. His openness to new possibilities is a much valued quality in publishers. And another colleague, Sandie Barnard, has helped with regular transfusions of enthusiasm. The poets I have been in contact with have been unfailingly polite and encouraging, and to all of them I extend my sincere gratitude. Finally, I am very pleased that a number of fellow parishioners, past and present, can join me in this project through their writing. And, among these, I am very grateful to Jane Watanabe for accepting the commission to paint a water-colour, details of which appear on the cover of this book. All of the above co-operation has helped to make the project, to my mind, a genuine collaboration.

David A. Kent
Feast of the Epiphany, 1988
Toronto

✠ 22

NOTES

1 Northrop Frye, "Conclusion," in *Literary History of Canada: Canadian Literature in English*, Gen. ed. Carl F. Klinck (Toronto: Univ. of Toronto Press, 1965), p. 832. Also, see (for example) Dennis Duffy, *Marshall McLuhan*, Canadian Writers Number 1 (Toronto: McClelland and Stewart, 1969), pp. 43–44.

2 For example, Jonathan Culler — a respected scholar of comparative literature — has lamented the "legitimation of religious discourse" by his own discipline; he evidently stands among those who "regard religion as a curious, irrelevant survival" ["Comparative Literature and the Pieties," *Profession* 86 (MLA), p. 31]. A response to Culler has been made by Roy Battenhouse, "Anti-Religion in Academia," *Christianity and Literature*, XXXVII, No. 1 (Fall, 1987), 7–22.

3 W.H. Auden, "Postscript: Christianity and Art," rpt. in *The New Orpheus: Essays Toward a Christian Poetic*, ed. Nathan A. Scott, Jr. (New York: Sheed and Ward, 1964), p. 76.

4 Isaac Disraeli, "Psalm Singing" in his *Curiousities of Literature*, New ed., ed. Benjamin Disraeli (London: Routledge, Warnes, and Routledge, 1859), II, 472.

5 Tim Lilburn, "Thoughts Towards a Christian Poetics," *Brick*, No. 29 (1987), p. 34.

6 Michael Edwards, *Towards a Christian Poetics* (Grand Rapids, Mich.: William B. Eerdmans, 1984), p. 150.

7 Marcia L. Colish, *The Mirror of Language: A Study in the Medieval Theory of Knowledge*, rev. ed. (Lincoln: Univ. of Nebraska Press, 1983), p. 26.

8 *The New Oxford Book of Christian Verse*, ed. Donald Davie (Oxford: Oxford Univ. Press, 1981), xx–xxi. For the view of hymns I follow, see Elizabeth Jennings, *Christian Poetry*, The Twentieth Century Encyclopedia of Catholicism, Vol. 118 (New York: Hawthorn Books, 1965), p. 12.

9 Margaret Avison, "Muse of Danger," *His* (March 1968), pp. 33–35; rpt. in *"Lighting Up the Terrain": The Poetry of Margaret Avison*, ed. David A. Kent (Toronto: ECW PRESS, 1987), p. 145.

Susanna Moodie

PARAPHRASE
PSALM XLIV

O Mighty God! our fathers told
  The wondrous works thou didst of yore;
Thy glories in the days of old,
  Wrought on proud Egypt's hostile shore.
Thy wrath swept through that guilty land;
  Before thy face the heathen fled;
His people, with an outstretched hand,
  The Lord of Hosts in triumph led!

It was not counsel, spear, nor sword,
  A heritage for Israel won;
It was Jehovah's awful word
  That led our conquering armies on.
The heathen host — their warriors brave —
  Were scattered when the Lord arose;
At his terrific glance, a grave
  Was found by Jacob's haughty foes!

God of our strength! Almighty Power!
  Our sure defence, our sword and shield,
Still guide our hosts in danger's hour,
  Still lead our armies to the field.
In thee we trust — what foe can stand
  The awful brightness of thine eye?
Both life and death are in thy hand,
  And in thy smile is victory!

John McPherson

PROBATION

We are here to redeem the fleeting time
  Of the few and evil days,
To journey in hope to the better clime
  On which the believing gaze.
We are here to encourage the lowly heart,
  To cherish the purer flame,
And to parry the wily tempter's dart
  With the shield of a righteous aim.

The future depends on the path we choose
  On the right of the race we run;
We have heaven's bright summit to gain or lose,
  We have hell's dark depths to shun.
Then such be our course that our friends may say
  At the close of our weary strife,
That we rest from the toil of our pilgrim-way
  In the land of eternal life.

OLD HANNAH

'Tis Sabbath morn, and a holy balm
  Drops down on the heart like dew,
And the sunbeam's gleam like a blessèd dream
  Afar on the mountains blue.
Old Hannah's by her cottage door,
  In her faded widow's cap;
She is sitting alone on the old grey stone,
  With the Bible in her lap.

An oak is hanging above her head,
  And the burn is wimpling by;
The primroses peep from their sylvan keep,
  And the lark is in the sky.
Beneath that shade her children played,
  But they're all away with Death,
And she sits alone on the old grey stone
  To hear what the Spirit saith.

Her years are past three score and ten,
  And her eyes are waxing dim,
But the page is bright with a living light,
  And her heart leaps up to Him
Who pours the mystic Harmony
  Which the soul alone can hear!
She is not alone on the old grey stone,
  Tho' no earthly friend is near.

There's no one left to love her now;
  But the Eye that never sleeps
Looks on her in love from the heavens above,
  And with quiet joy she weeps.
For she feels the balm of bliss is poured
  In her lone heart's sorest spot:
The widow lone on the old grey stone
  Has a peace the world knows not.

Charles Sangster

MY PRAYER

O God! forgive the erring thought,
  The erring word and deed,
And in thy mercy hear the Christ
  Who comes to intercede.

My sins, like mountain-weights of lead,
  Weigh heavy on my soul;
I'm bruised and broken in this strife,
  But Thou canst make me whole.

Allay this fever of unrest,
  That fights against the Will;
And in Thy still small voice do Thou
  But whisper, "Peace, be still!"

Until within this heart of mine
  Thy lasting peace come down,
Will all the waves of Passion roll,
  Each good resolve to drown.

We walk in blindness and dark night
  Through half of our earthly way;
Our clouds of weaknesses obscure
  The glory of the day.

We cannot lead the lives we would,
  But grope in dumb amaze,
Leaving the straight and flowery paths
  To tread the crooked ways.

We are as pilgrims toiling on
  Through all the weary hours;
And our poor hands are torn with thorns,
  Plucking life's tempting flowers.

We worship at a thousand shrines,
  And build upon the sands,
Passing the one great Temple, and
  The Rock on which it stands.

O, fading dream of human life!
  What can this change portend?
I long for higher walks, and true
  Progression without end.

Here I know nothing, and my search
  Can find no secret out;
I cannot think a single thought
  That is not mixed with doubt.

Relying on the higher source,
  The influence divine,
I can but hope that light may dawn
  Within this soul of mine.

I ask not wisdom, such as that
  To which the world is prone,
Nor knowledge ask, unless it come
  Direct from God alone.

Send down then, God! in mercy send
  Thy Love and Truth to me,
That I may henceforth walk in light
  That comes direct from Thee.

SONNET III

Oh, holy sabbath morn! thrice blessed day
Of solemn rest, true peace, and earnest prayer.
How many hearts that never knelt to pray
Are glad to breathe thy soul-sustaining air.
I sit within the quiet woods, and hear
The village church-bell's soft inviting sound,
And to the confines of the loftiest sphere
Imagination wings its airy round;
A myriad spirits have assembled there,
Whose prayers on earth a sweet acceptance found.
I go to worship in Thy House, O God!
With her, thy young creation bright and fair;
Help us to do Thy will, and not despair,
Though both our hearts should bend beneath Thy
    chastening rod.

IN AN ALBUM

Angel bright that walks beside her,
    Guide her steps from day to day,
Rippling down the light celestial
    On the head of Christian May.

Light that shines through all the darkness
    Of the weariest mortal way,
Permeate, keep pure the spirit,
    And the heart, of Christian May.

Light that never pales its radiance,
    Light that never leads astray,
Up her good deeds' golden ladder
    Speed the steps of Christian May.

Till thy lips, O Guardian-Angel,
    Joining in the welcome lay,
Sing the Anthem of Rejoicing
    With the Soul of Christian May.

Thomas D'Arcy McGee

THE THREE SISTERS

I

There are three angel sisters
  That haunt the open sea,
Three loving, life-like sisters,
  Though different they be.

II

One lifts her brow, like morning,
  Above the waters dark,
And the star that brow adorning
  Laves many a beaten bark.

III

One, by her anchor clinging,
  Walks the waters, like our Lord,
And the song she still is singing
  The dead to life hath stirr'd.

IV

But of all the angel sisters
  Who haunt the open sea,
The fondest and the fairest,
  Sweet Saint Charity for me.

V

Her spirit fires the coldest,
  And arms the weakest heart;
When death hath seized the boldest,
  The burial is her part.

VI

On a thousand giddy headlands
  Her fleeting robe is seen;
By a thousand bays her buried
  Calmly rest beneath the green.

VII

She hath no star nor anchor,
  Nor lofty look hath she,
But of all the angelic sisters,
  Sweet Saint Charity for me!

Mrs. J. C. Yule

LIVING AND DYING

Living for Christ, I die; — how strange, that I,
Thus dying, live, — and yet, thus living, die!
Living for Christ, I die; — yet, wondrous thought,
In that same death a deathless life is wrought; —
Living, I die to Earth, to self, to sin; —
Oh, blessed death, in which such life I win!

Dying for Christ, I live! — death cannot be
A terror, then, to one from death set free!
Living for Christ, rich blessings I attain;
Yet, dying for Him, mine is greater gain!
Life for my Lord, is death to sin and strife,
Yet death for Him is everlasting life!

Dying for Christ, I live! — and yet, not I,
But He lives in me, who did for me die.
I die to live; — He lives to die no more,
Who, in His death my own death-sentence bore!
"To live is Christ," if Christ within me reign;
To die more blessed, since "to die is gain!"

Edward Hartley Dewart

LEAD THOU ME ON

Lead Thou me on. My path is steep:
Beset with foes I cannot see —
Father thy child in safety keep,
      My strength is all from Thee.

When clouds and darkness round me close,
And fierce temptations sorely press,
Hold Thou my hand; repel my foes;
      With calm endurance bless.

Forgive my weak, distrustful fears;
Let thankful love my portion be,
Till, safe from conflicts, doubts, and tears,
      I rest above with Thee.

Mrs. Rosanna Leprohon

THE STABLE OF BETHLEHEM

'Twas not a palace proud and fair
  He chose for His first home;
No dazz'ling pile of grandeur rare,
  With pillar'd hall and dome;
Oh no! a stable, rude and poor,
  Received Him at His birth;
And thus was born, unknown, obscure,
  The Lord of Heaven and Earth.

No band of anxious menials there,
  To tend the new-born child,
Joseph alone and Mary fair
  Upon the infant smiled;
No broidered linens fine had they
  Those little limbs to fold,
No baby garments rich and gay,
  No tissues wrought with gold.

Come to your Saviour's lowly bed,
  Ye vain and proud of heart!
And learn with bowed and humbled head
  The lesson 'twill impart;
'Twill teach you not to prize too high
  The riches vain of earth —
But to lay up God's bright sky
  Treasures of truer worth.

And you, poor stricken sons of grief,
  Sad outcasts of this life,
Come, too, and seek a sure relief
  For your heart's bitter strife;
Enter that village stable door,
  And view that lowly cot —
Will it not teach you to endure,
  And even bless your lot?

Mary Herbert

STANZAS

"Speak, Lord, for thy servant heareth."

Speak, gracious Lord, for my sad heart
  Refuses every voice but thine;
Descend, and heavenly balm impart,
  Oh, Comforter divine!

This solemn night, those glittering stars,
  Tell of Thy majesty and power;
But something more I ask, I crave,
  At this deep midnight hour.

I ask a token of Thy love, —
  The "still, small voice" I wait to hear,
Oh, speak, — and hope and joy shall spring,
  My fainting heart to cheer.

Emblem of death, its sombre peace,
  This gloom, this silence, seems to me;
How shrink life's vanities before
  Awful eternity!

While from the "better land" methinks,
  Sweet, earnest voices call me,
Solemn their tones, yet full of love,
  They breathe alone of Thee.

And countless memories of the past,
  Strengthen my faith and nerve my heart;
The mercy Thou to them hast shown,
  Shall ne'er from me depart.

Therefore, confiding in Thy love,
  In sleep, my weary eyes I close,
Lulled by the gentle voice of peace,
  Into a deep repose.

John Reade

THE PRODIGAL'S RETURN

(St. Luke's Gospel, xv. 17–32)

I

Long, my Father, have I wandered
  From the home I loved of old, —
All Thy tender mercies squandered,
  All Thy loving-kindness sold.

II

I have sinned against Thy goodness,
  Mocked Thy sorrow, scorned Thy love;
Treated all Thy care with rudeness,
  'Gainst Thy gentle Spirit strove.

III

Far from Thy free, bounteous table,
  I have fed on husks of sin;
Wayward, thankless, and unstable,
  Father, will Thou take me in?

IV

Take me, oh! in mercy take me,
  To Thy blessed home again,
And let no enticement shake me, —
  Satan's wiles nor wicked men.

V

I am sinful, doubting, fearing —
  Thou canst banish all alarm;
I am weak, and blind, and erring —
  Thou canst shield from every harm.

VI

Look upon me, crushed and broken,
  Humble, contrite, at Thy feet.
Dost Thou know me? Hast Thou spoken?
  "Hast Thou come Thy child to meet!"

VII

Lost and found! Once dead, now living!
  Once an outcast, now a son!
Once despairing, now believing, —
  I my Father's house have won.

Isabella Valancy Crawford

HIS CLAY

He died; he was buried, the last of his race,
And they laid him away in his burial-place.

And he said in his will, "When I have done
With the mask of clay that I have on,

"Bury it simply — I'm done with it,
At best is only a poor misfit.

"It cramped my brains and chained my soul,
And it clogged my feet as I sought my goal.

"When my soul and I were inclined to shout
O'er some noble thought we had chiselled out;

"When we'd polished the marble until it stood
So fair that we truly said: ' 'Tis good!'

"My soul would tremble, my spirit quail,
For it fell to the flesh to uplift the veil.

"It took our thought in its hands of clay,
And lo! how the beauty had passed away.

"When Love came in to abide with me,
I said, 'Welcome, Son of Eternity!'

"I built him an altar strong and white,
Such as might stand in God's own sight;

"I chanted his glorious litany —
Pure Love is the Son of Eternity;

"But ever my altar shook alway
'Neath the brute hands of the tyrant clay.

"Its voice, with its accents harsh and drear,
Mocked at my soul and wailed in its ear:

" 'Why tend the altar and bend the knee?
Love lives and dies in the dust with me.'

So the flesh that I wore chanced ever to be
Less of my friend than my enemy.

"Is there a moment this death-strong earth
Thrills, and remembers her time of birth?

"Is there a time when she knows her clay
As a star in the coil of the astral way?

"Who may tell? But the soul in its clod
Knows in swift moments its kinship to God —

"Quick lights in its chambers that flicker alway
Before the hot breath of the tyrant clay.

"So the flesh that I wore chanced ever to be
Less of my friend than my enemy.

"So bury it deeply — strong foe, weak friend —
And bury it cheaply, — and there its end!"

Sir Charles G. D. Roberts

A CHILD'S PRAYER AT EVENING

(Domine, cui sunt Pleiades curae)

Father, who keepest
  The stars in Thy care,
Me, too, Thy little one,
  Childish in prayer,
Keep, as Thou keepest
  The soft night through,
Thy long, white lilies
  Asleep in Thy dew.

How long it was I did not know,
  That I had waited, watched, and feared.
It seemed a thousand years ago
  The last pale lights had disappeared.
I knew the place was a narrow room
Up, up beyond the reach of doom.

Then came a light more red than flame; —
  No sun-dawn, but the soul laid bare
Of earth and sky and sea became
  A presence burning everywhere;
And I was glad my narrow room
Was high above the reach of doom.

Windows there were in either wall,
  Deep cleft, and set with radiant glass,
Wherethrough I watched the mountains fall,
  The ages wither up and pass.
I knew their doom could never climb
My tower beyond the tops of Time.

A sea of faces then I saw,
  Of men who had been, men long dead.
Figured with dreams of joy and awe
  The heavens unrolled in lambent red;
While far below the faces cried —
'Give us the dream for which we died!'

Ever the woven shapes rolled by
  Above the faces hungering.
With quiet and incurious eye
  I noted many a wondrous thing, —
Seas of clear glass, and singing streams,
In that high pageantry of dreams;

Cities of sard and chrysoprase
  Where choired Hosannas never cease;
Valhallas of celestial frays,
  And lotus-pools of endless peace;
But still the faces gaped and cried —
'Give us the dream for which we died!'

At length my quiet heart was stirred,
  Hearing them cry so long in vain.
But while I listened for a word
  That should translate them from their pain,
I saw that here and there a face
Shone, and was lifted from its place.

And flashed into the moving dome
  An ecstasy of prismed fire.
And then said I, 'A soul has come
  To the deep zenith of desire!'
But still I wondered if it knew
The dream for which it died was true.

I wondered — who shall say how long?
  (One heart-beat? — Thrice ten thousand years?)
Till suddenly there was no throng
  Of faces to arraign the spheres, —
No more white faces there to cry
To those great pageants of the sky.

Then quietly I grew aware
  Of one who came with eyes of bliss
And brow of calm and lips of prayer.
  Said I — 'How wonderful is this!
Where are the faces once that cried —
'Give us the dream for which we died'?'

The answer fell as soft as sleep, —
  'I am of those who, having cried
So long in that tumultuous deep,
  Have won the dream for which we died.'
And then said I — 'Which dream was true?
For many were revealed to you!'

He answered — 'To the soul made wise
  All true, all beautiful they seem.
But the white peace that fills our eyes
  Outdoes desire, outreaches dream.
For we are come unto the place
Where always we behold God's face!'

ASCRIPTION

O Thou who hast beneath Thy hand
The dark foundations of the land, —
The motion of whose ordered thought
An instant universe hath wrought, —

Who hast within Thine equal heed
The rolling sun, the ripening seed,
The azure of the speedwell's eye,
The vast solemnities of sky, —

Who hear'st no less the feeble note
Of one small bird's awakening throat,
Than that unnamed, tremendous chord
Arcturus sounds before his Lord, —

More sweet to Thee than all acclaim
Of storm and ocean, stars and flame,
In favour more before Thy face
Than pageantry of time and space,

The worship and the service be
Of him Thou madest most like Thee, —
Who in his nostrils hath Thy breath,
Whose spirit is the Lord of death!

TO A CERTAIN MYSTIC

Sometimes you saw what others could not see.
  Sometimes you heard what no one else could hear: —
A light beyond the unfathomable dark,
  A voice that sounded only to your ear.

And did you, voyaging the tides of vision
  In your lone shallop, steering by what star,
Catch hints of some Elysian fragrance, wafted
  On winds impalpable, from who knows how far?

And did dawn show you driftage from strange continents
  Of which we dream but no man surely knows, —
Some shed gold leafage from the Tree Eternal,
  Some petals of the Imperishable Rose?

And did you once, Columbus of the spirit,
  Essay the crossing of that unknown sea,
Really touch land beyond the mists of rumour
  And find new lands where they were dreamed to be?

Ah, why brought you not back the word of power,
  The charted course, the unambiguous sign,
Or even some small seed, whence we might grow
  A flower unmistakably divine?

But you came empty-handed, and your tongue
  Babbled strange tidings none could wholly trust.
And if we half believed you, it was only
  Because we would, and not because we must.

Archibald Lampman

NEW YEAR'S EVE

Once on the year's last eve in my mind's might
    Sitting in dreams, not sad, nor quite elysian,
    Balancing all 'twixt wonder and derision,
Methought my body and all this world took flight,
And vanished from me, as a dream, outright;
    Leaning out thus in sudden strange decision,
    I saw as in the flashing of a vision,
Far down between the tall towers of the night,
    Borne by great winds in awful unison,
        The teeming masses of mankind sweep by,
        Even as a glittering river with deep sound
    And innumerable banners, rolling on,
        Over the starry border-glooms that bound
        The last gray space in dim eternity.

And all that strange unearthly multitude
    Seemed twisted in vast seething companies,
    That evermore, with hoarse and terrible cries
And desperate encounter at mad feud,
Plunged onward, each in its implacable mood
    Borne down over the trampled blazonries
    Of other faiths and other phantasies,
Each following furiously, and each pursued;
    So sped they on with tumult vast and grim,
        But ever meseemed beyond them I could see
        White-haloed groups that sought perpetually
        The figure of one crowned and sacrificed;
    And faint, far forward, floating tall and dim,
        The banners of our Lord and Master, Christ.

THE MARTYRS

O ye, who found in men's brief ways no sign
   Of strength or help, so cast them forth, and threw
   Your whole souls up to one ye deemed most true,
Nor failed nor doubted but held fast your line,
Seeing before you that divine face shine;
   Shall we not mourn, when yours are now so few,
   Those sterner days, when all men yearned to you,
White souls whose beauty made their world divine:
Yet still across life's tangled storms we see,
   Following the cross, your pale procession led,
   One hope, one end, all others sacrificed,
Self-abnegation, love, humility,
   Your faces shining toward the bended head,
   The wounded hands and patient feet of Christ.

VIRTUE

I deem that virtue but a thing of straw
That is not self-subsistent, needs the press
Of sharp-eyed custom, or the point of law
To teach it honour, justice, gentleness.
His soul is but a shadow who does well
Through lure of gifts or terror of the rod,
Some painted paradise or pictured hell,
Not for the love but for the fear of God.

Him only do I honour in whom right,
Not the sour product of some grudged control,
Flows from a Godlike habit, whose clear soul,
Bathed in the noontide of an inward light,
In its own strength and beauty is secure,
Too proud to lie, too proud to be impure.

ALCYONE

I have had glimpses of thy way,
   And moved with winds and walked with stars,
But, weary, I have fallen astray,
   And, wounded, who shall count my scars?

O Master, all my strength is gone;
   Unto the very earth I bow;
I have no light to lead me on;
   With aching heart and burning brow,
I lie as one that travaileth
In sorrow more than he can bear;
I sit in darkness as of death,
   And scatter dust upon my hair.

The God within my soul hath slept,
   And I have shamed the nobler rule;
O Master, I have whined and crept;
   O Spirit, I have played the fool.
Like him of old upon whose head
   His follies hung in dark arrears,
I groan and travail in my bed,
   And water it with bitter tears.

I stand upon thy mountain-heads,
And gaze until mine eyes are dim;
The golden morning glows and spreads;
   The hoary vapours break and swim.
I see thy blossoming fields, divine,
   Thy shining clouds, thy blessed trees —
And then that broken soul of mine —
   How much less beautiful than these!

Pauline Johnson

CHRISTMASTIDE

I may not go to-night to Bethlehem,
Nor follow star-directed ways, nor tread
The paths wherein the shepherds walked, that led
To Christ, and peace, and God's good will to men.

I may not hear the Herald Angel's song
Peal through the Oriental skies, nor see
The wonder of that Heavenly company
Announce the King the world had waited long.

The manager throne I may not kneel before,
Or see how man to God is reconciled,
Through pure St. Mary's purer, holier child;
The human Christ these eyes may not adore.

I may not carry frankincense and myrrh
With adoration to the Holy One;
Nor gold have I to give the Perfect Son,
To be with those wise kings a worshipper.

Not mine the joy that Heaven sent to them,
For ages since Time swung and locked his gates,
But I may kneel without — the star still waits
To guide me on to holy Bethlehem.

BRIER

Because, dear Christ, your tender, wounded arm
   Bends back the brier that edges life's long way
That no hurt comes to heart, to soul no harm,
   I do not feel the thorns so much to-day.

Because I never knew your care to tire,
   Your hand to weary guiding me aright,
Because you walk before and crush the brier,
   It does not pierce my feet so much to-night.

Because so often you have hearkened to
   My selfish prayers, I ask but one thing now,
That these harsh hands of mine add not unto
   The crown of thorns upon your bleeding brow.

A PRODIGAL

My heart forgot its God for love of you,
   And you forgot me, other loves to learn;
Now through a wilderness of thorn and rue
   Back to my God I turn.

And just because my God forgets the past,
   And in forgetting does not ask to know
Why I once left His arms for yours, at last
   Back to my God I go.

THE WAYSIDE CROSS

A wayside cross at set of day
Unto my spirit thus did say —

'O soul, my branching arms you see
Point four ways to infinity.

'One points to infinite above,
To show the height of heavenly love.

'Two point to infinite width, which shows
That heavenly love no limit knows.

'One points to infinite beneath,
To show God's love is under death.

'The four arms join, an emblem sweet
That in God's heart all loves will meet.'

I thanked the cross as I turned away
For such sweet thoughts in the twilight grey.

THE SNOWSTORM

The sky is hid in a snowy shroud,
  And the road in the woods is white,
But the dear God watches above the cloud
      In the centre of light.

In the woods is the hush of the snowflakes' fall,
  And the creak of a lumberman's sleigh,
But in Heaven the choirs of the Master of all
      Make praise alway.

Up there is the throne of the Triune God
  And the worshipping multitudes,
And here is the long white winter road
      And the silent woods.

'IN TE, DOMINE'

The hills may crumble into dust,
  The earth may swallow up the sea,
But naught can shake my living trust
  In Him whose firm hands moulded me.

For when I draw myself apart
  From things which make my vision dim,
Deep in the silence of my heart
  He meets me, and I speak with Him.

A SISTER OF CHARITY

She made a nunnery of her life,
  Plain duties hedged it round,
No echoes of the outer strife
  Could reach its hallowed ground.

Her rule was simple as her creed,
  She tried to do each day
Some act of kindness that might speed
  A sad soul on its way.

She had no wealth, and yet she made
  So many rich at heart;
Her lot was hidden, yet she played
  No inconspicuous part.

Some wondered men had passed her by,
  Some said she would not wed,
I think the secret truth must lie
  Long buried with the dead.

That cheery smile, that gentle touch,
  That heart so free from stain,
Could have no other source but such
  As lies in conquered pain.

All living creatures loved her well,
  And blessed the ground she trod;
The pencillings in her Bible tell
  Her communing with God.

And when the call came suddenly,
  And sleep preceded death,
There was no struggle we could see,
  No hard and laboured breath.

Gently as dawn, the end drew nigh;
  Her life had been so sweet,
I think she did not need to die
  To reach the Master's feet.

REQUIESCANT

In lonely watches night by night,
Great visions burst upon my sight,
For down the stretches of the sky
The hosts of dead go marching by.

Strange ghostly banners o'er them float,
Strange bugles sound an awful note,
And all their faces and their eyes
Are lit with starlight from the skies.

The anguish and the pain have passed
And peace hath come to them at last,
But in the stern looks linger still
The iron purpose and the will.

Dear Christ, who reign'st above the flood
Of human tears and human blood,
A weary road these men have trod,
O house them in the home of God.

In a field near Ypres.
April 1915

MEDITATION AT PERUGIA

The sunset colours mingle in the sky,
  And over all the Umbrian valleys flow;
  Trevi is touched with wonder, and the glow
Finds high Perugia crimson with renown;
    Spello is bright;
And, ah! St. Francis, thy deep-treasured town,
    Enshrined Assisi, fully fronts the light.

This valley knew thee many a year ago;
  Thy shrine was built by simpleness of heart;
  And from the wound called life thou drew'st the smart:
Unquiet kings came to thee and the sad poor —
    Thou gavest them peace;
Far as the Sultan and the Iberian shore
    Thy faith and abnegation gave release.

Deeper our faith, but not so sweet as thine;
  Wider our view, but not so sanely sure;
  For we are troubled by the witching lure
Of Science, with her lightning on the mist;
    Science that clears,
Yet never quite discloses what she wist,
    And leaves us half with doubts and half with fears.

We act her dreams that shadow forth the truth,
  That somehow here the very nerves of God
  Thrill the old fires, the rocks, the primal sod;
We throw our speech upon the open air,
    And it is caught
Far down the world, to sing and murmur there;
  Our common words are with deep wonder fraught.

Shall not the subtle spirit of man contrive
  To charm the tremulous ether of the soul,
  Wherein it breathes? — until, from pole to pole,
Those who are kin shall speak, as face to face,
    From star to star,
Even from earth to the mòst secret place,
      Where God and the supreme archangels are.

Shall we not prove, what thou hast faintly taught,
  That all the powers of earth and air are one,
  That one deep law persists from mole to sun?
Shall we not search the heart of God and find
    That law empearled,
Until all things that are in matter and mind
    Throb with the secret that began the world?

Yea, we have journeyed since thou trod'st the road,
  Yet still we keep the foreappointed quest;
  While the last sunset smoulders in the West,
Still the great faith with the undying hope
    Upsprings and flows,
While dim Assisi fades on the wide slope
    And the deep Umbrian valleys fill with rose.

J. E. H. MacDonald

GALLOWS AND CROSS

I saw one hung upon a cross
That every man might see
If sinless God could pardon sin
All men might pardoners be.

I saw the gallows lifted high
And in the cruel rope
The twisted law and sin of man
Strangled the Saviour's hope.

I heard a tortured spirit cry
Upon the darkened cross;
And heavy was the lowered sky
With sin and pain and loss.

THE MANGER

Not only far in Bethlehem
The Christ was born that olden day
His birth-cry comes within the heart
That opens Him the way.

There is a manger in the soul
Where groping longings champ and pull
And in the heedless town without
The glittering inns are full.

O Mary of the holy smile
To my warm quietness repair
Soothe thy dear child in lowliness
That I may tend Him there.

E. J. Pratt

FROM STONE TO STEEL

From stone to bronze, from bronze to steel
Along the road-dust of the sun,
Two revolutions of the wheel
From Java to Geneva run.

The snarl Neanderthal is worn
Close to the smiling Aryan lips,
The civil polish of the horn
Gleams from our praying finger tips.

The evolution of desire
Has but matured a toxic wine,
Drunk long before its heady fire
Reddened Euphrates or the Rhine.

Between the temple and the cave
The boundary lies tissue-thin:
The yearlings still the altars crave
As satisfaction for a sin.

The road goes up, the road goes down —
Let Java or Geneva be —
But whether to the cross or crown,
The path lies through Gethsemane.

THE DEPRESSION ENDS

If I could take within my hand
The rod of Prospero for an hour,
With space and speed at my command,
And astro-physics in my power,
Having no reason for my scheme
Beyond the logic of a dream
To change a world predestinate
From the eternal loom of fate,
I'd realize my mad chimera
By smashing distaff and the spinner,
And usher in the golden era
With an apocalyptic dinner.
I'd place a table in the skies
No earthly mind could visualize:
No instruments of earth could bound it —
'Twould take the light-years to go round it.
And to this feast I would invite
Only the faithful, the elect —
The shabby ones of earth's despite,
The victims of her rude neglect,
The most unkempt and motley throng
Ever described in tale or song.
All the good lads I've ever known
From the twelve winds of sea and land
Should hear my shattering bugle tone
And feel its summoning command.
No one should come who never knew
A famine day of rationed gruel,
Nor heard his stomach like a flue
Roaring with wind instead of fuel:
No self-made men who proudly claim
To be the architects of fame; —
No profiteers whose double chins
Are battened on the Corn-Exchange,
While continental breadlines range
Before the dust of flour-bins.
These shall not enter, nor shall those
Who soured with the sun complain
Of all their manufactured woes,
Yet never had an honest pain:
Not these — the well-groomed and the sleeked,

But all the gaunt, the cavern-cheeked,
The waifs whose tightened belts declare
The thinness of their daily fare;
The ill-starred from their natal days,
The gaffers and the stowaways,
The road-tramps and the alley-bred
Who leap to scraps that others fling,
With luck less than the Tishbite's, fed
On manna from the raven's wing.

This dinner, now years overdue,
Shall centre in a barbecue.
Orion's club — no longer fable —
Shall fall upon the Taurus head.
No less than Centaurs shall be led
In roaring pairs forth from their stable
And harnessed to the Wain to pull
The mighty carcass of the bull
Across the tundras to the table,
Where he shall stretch from head to stern,
Roasted and basted to a turn.
I'd have the Pleiades prepare
Jugged Lepus (to the vulgar *hare*),
Galactic venison just done
From the corona of the sun,
Hoof jellies from Monoceros,
Planked tuna, shad, stewed terrapin,
And red-gut salmon captured in
The deltas of the Southern Cross.
Devilled shrimps, and scalloped clams,
Flamingoes, capons, luscious yams
And cherries from Hesperides;
And every man and every beast,
Known to the stars' directories
For speed of foot and strength of back,
Would be the couriers to this feast —
Mercury, Atlas, Hercules,
Each bearing a capacious pack.
I would conscript the Gemini,
Persuading Castor to compete
With Pollux on a heavy wager,
Buckboard against the sled, that he,
With Capricornus could not beat

His brother mushing Canis Major.
And on the journey there I'd hail
Aquarius with his nets and pail,
And Neptune with his prong to meet us
At some point on the shores of Cetus,
And bid them superintend a cargo
Of fresh sea-food upon the Argo —
Sturgeon and shell-fish that might serve
To fill the side-boards with *hors d'œuvres*.

And worthy of the banquet spread
Within this royal court of night,
A curving canopy of light
Shall roof it myriad-diamonded.
For high above the table head
Shall sway a candelabrum where,
According to the legend, dwelt a
Lady seated in a chair
With Alpha, Beta, Gamma, Delta,
Busy braiding up her hair.
Sirius, the dog-star, shall be put
Immediately above the foot,
And central from the cupola
Shall hang the cluster — Auriga,
With that deep sapphire-hearted stella,
The loveliest of the lamps, Capella.

For all old men whose pilgrim feet
Were calloused with life's dust and heat,
Whose throats were arid with its thirst,
I'd smite Jove's taverns till they burst,
And punch the spigots of his vats,
Till flagons, kegs and barrels all
Were drained of their ambroisal
As dry as the Sahara flats.
For toothless, winded ladies who,
Timid and hesitating, fear
They might not stand the barbecue
(Being so near their obsequies),
I'd serve purees fresh from the ear
Of Spica with a mild ragout —
To satisfy the calories —
Of breast of Cygnus stiffened by

The hind left leg of Aries,
As a last wind-up before they die.
And I would have no wardens there,
Searching the platters for a reason
To seize Diana and declare
That venison is out of season.
For all those children hunger-worn
From drought or flood and harvest failing,
Whether from Nile or Danube hailing,
Or Yangtze or the Volga born,
I'd communize the total yields
Of summer in the Elysian fields,
Gather the berries from the shrubs
To crown soufflés and syllabubs.

Dumplings and trifles and *éclaires*
And roly-polies shall be theirs;
Search as you may, you will not find
One dash of oil, one dish of prunes
To spoil the taste of the macaroons,
And I would have you bear in mind
No dietic aunt-in-law,
With hook-nose and prognathic jaw,
Will try her vain reducing fads
Upon these wenches and these lads.
Now that these grand festivities
Might start with holy auspices,
I would select with Christian care,
To offer up the vesper prayer,
A padre of high blood — no white
Self-pinched, self-punished anchorite,
Who credits up against his dying
His boasted hours of mortifying,
Who thinks he hears a funeral bell
In dinner gongs on principle.
He shall be left to mourn this night,
Walled in his dim religious light:
Unto this feast he shall not come
To breathe his gloom. No! rather some
Sagacious and expansive friar,
Who beams good-will, who loves a briar,
Who, when he has his fellows with him
Around a board, can make a grace

Sonorous, full of liquid rhythm,
Boom from his lungs' majestic bass;
Who, when requested by his host
To do the honours to a toast,
Calls on the clan to rise and hold
Their glasses to the light a minute,
Just to observe the mellow gold
And the rare glint of autumn in it.

Now even at this hour he stands,
The benison upon his face,
In his white hair and moulded hands,
No less than in his spoken grace.
"We thank thee for this table spread
In such a hall, on such a night,
With such unusual stores of bread,
O Lord of love! O Lord of light!
We magnify thy name in praise
At what thy messengers have brought,
For not since Galilean days
Has such a miracle been wrought.
The guests whom thou hast bidden come,
The starved, the maimed, the deaf, and dumb,
Were misfits in a world of evil,
And ridden hard by man and devil.
The seven years they have passed through
Were leaner than what Israel knew.
Dear Lord, forgive my liberty,
In telling what thou mayst not know,
For it must seem so queer to thee,
What happens on our earth below:
The sheep graze on a thousand hills,
The cattle roam upon the plains,
The cotton waits upon the mills,
The stores are bursting with their grains,
And yet these ragged ones that kneel
To take thy grace before their meal
Are said to be thy chosen ones,
Lord of the planets and the suns!
Therefore let thy favours fall
In rich abundance on them all.
May not one stomach here to-night
Turn traitor on its appetite.

Take under thy peculiar care
The infants and the aged. Bestow
Upon all invalids a rare
Release of their digestive flow,
That they, with health returned, may know
A hunger equal to the fare,
And for these mercies, Lord, we'll praise
Thee to the limit of our days."

He ended. The salubrious feast
Began: with inundating mirth
It drowned all memories of earth:
It quenched the midnight chimes: nor ceased
It till the wand of Prospero,
Turning its magic on the east,
Broke on a master charm, when lo!
Answering the summons of her name,
Fresh from the surf of Neptune came
Aurora to the Portico.

CYCLES

There was a time we knew our foes,
Could recognize their features well,
Name them before we bartered blows;
So in our challenges could tell
What the damned quarrel was about,
As with our fists we slugged it out.

When distance intervened, the call
Of trumpets sped the spear and arrow;
From stone and sling to musket ball
The path was blasted to the marrow;
But still we kept our foes in sight,
Dusk waiting for the morning light.

We need no more that light of day,
No need of faces to be seen;
The squadrons in the skies we slay
Through moving shadows on a screen:
By nailing echoes under sea
We kill with like geometry.

Now since the Lord of Love is late
In being summoned to the ring
To keep in bounds the range of hate,
The Lord of Hosts to whom we sing
As Marshal of both man and brute
May be invoked as substitute.

Whether from heaven or from hell,
May he return as referee,
And, keen-eared to an honest bell,
Splitting the foul from fair, feel free
To send us forth into the lists,
Armed only with our naked fists.

And then before our voice is dumb,
Before our blood-shot eyes go blind,
The Lord of Love and Life may come
To lead our ebbing veins to find
Enough for their recovery
Of plasma from Gethsemane.

Marjorie Pickthall

PÈRE LALEMENT

I lift the Lord on high,
Under the murmuring hemlock boughs, and see
The small birds of the forest lingering by
And making melody.
These are mine acolytes and these my choir,
And this mine altar in the cool green shade,
Where the wild soft-eyed does draw nigh
Wondering, as in the byre
Of Bethlehem the oxen heard Thy cry
And saw Thee, unafraid.

My boatmen sit apart,
Wolf-eyed, wolf-sinewed, stiller than the trees.
Help me, O Lord, for very slow of heart
And hard of faith are these.
Cruel are they, yet thy children. Foul are they,
Yet wert Thou born to save them utterly.
Then make me as I pray
Just to their hates, kind to their sorrows, wise
After their speech, and strong before their free
Indomitable eyes.

Do the French lilies reign
Over Mount Royal and Stadacona still?
Up the St. Lawrence comes the spring again,
Crowning each southward hill
And blossoming pool with beauty, while I roam
Far from the perilous folds that are my home,
There where we built St. Ignace for our needs,
Shaped the rough roof tree, turned the first
    sweet sod,
St. Ignace and St. Louis, little beads
On the rosary of God.

Pines shall Thy pillars be,
Fairer than those Sidonian cedars brought
By Hiram out of Tyre, and each birch-tree
Shines like a holy thought.
But come no worshippers; shall I confess,
St. Francis-like, the birds of the wilderness?
O, with Thy love my lonely head uphold.
A wandering shepherd I, who hath no sheep;
A wandering soul, who hath no scrip, nor gold,
Nor anywhere to sleep.

My hour of rest is done;
On the smooth ripple lifts the long canoe;
The hemlocks murmur sadly as the sun
Slants his dim arrows through.
Whither I go I know not, nor the way,
Dark with strange passions, vexed with
    heathen charms,
Holding I know not what of life or death;
Only be Thou beside me day by day,
Thy rod my guide and comfort, underneath
Thy everlasting arms.

SALUTARIS HOSTIA

When the moon is last awake,
Silver-thin above the fields,
Crushed, like roses, for Thy sake,
All my soul its fragrance yields.
All my hungry heart is fed
Sundering sweetness like a sword,
O my Lord,
Hidden within Thy broken bread.

Hands of morning, take the cup
Whence the Life of Love is drained;
Hold it, raise it, lift it up
Till the lucent heavens be stained.
Joy and sorrow, lip to lip,
Lost in likeness at the end,
O my Friend,
Taste Thy wine of fellowship.

All life's splendour, all life's pride,
Dust are they. I lay them down.
They were thorns that when You died
Wove for You a wounding crown.
But the brier of death's in bud,
All its loveliness he knows,
Sharon's Rose,
That has shared Thy flesh and blood.

DEUS MISEREATUR

Pleasant the ways whereon our feet were led,
Sweet the young hills, the valleys of content,
But now the hours of dew and dream have fled.
Lord we are spent.

We did not heed Thy warning in the skies,
We have not heard Thy voice nor known Thy fold;
But now the world is darkening to our eyes,
Lord, we grow old.

Now the sweet stream turns bitter with our tears,
Now dies the star we followed in the west,
Now are we sad and ill at ease with years,
Lord we would rest.

Lo, our proud lamps are emptied of their light,
Weary our hands to toil, our feet to roam;
Our day is past and swiftly falls Thy night.
Lord, lead us home.

Kenneth Leslie

LOVE SEEKS HIS BONDAGE

to Liam Fitzgibbon

Our victory comes not in listless fashion,
passions warp always to a fiercer passion,
the jungle cuts across no law of life,
our peace is bought there too with coin of strife,
love seeks his bondage, nor can life be found
where love with earth is not forever bound.
The grass cut down may guess why Jesus died,
the hooked fish may portend the Crucified.
We must ascend where dwell the lost and lowly
to find the single-heart, the pure, the holy,
there shall a common buttercup be best
to tell the golden-hearted from the rest,
there shall a blade of grass be sword of steel
dividing those who hurt from those who heal,
there what seemed lost is found and satisfied
to find a need its worth, a cross its pride.
The soul is nothing you can lay away
in lavender against a wedding day,
the soul is more than breath, it is a seed,
the human heart its garden and its need,
it must go out and drench itself in rain,
girdle itself with ground, it must know pain,
it must be trapped before it can be free
to flame, a rose, or stand up tall, a tree.

PEACE IS PASSION

To Nora

The river's peace is in its flowing,
the traveller's peace is in his going,
peace is passion unrestrained.

Rather hate and riding death
than quick eye and bated breath,
peace is carefulness disdained.

Love, to hold its own dear law,
found true peace on Golgotha.
Peace is loving uncontained.

JESUS THOUGHT LONG

Jesus thought long
   on an oar thinned to breaking.
It was flesh in His hands
   of hard toil partaking.
Jesus found beauty
   in the curl of a shaving
And truth in a yoke
   worn out and past saving.

EVANGEL

to Ervin Gaede

Where did the love of Jesus go
after he left us here below?

Into the hearts that hated him,
into the spears that baited him,
into the scorn of the Pharisee,
into the cross of Calvary,
straight to the citadel of fear,
blunting the point of the Roman spear,
rusting the sword in its noisy sheath,
lacing with thorns the Augustan wreath,
through eyes of Stephen to soul of Saul,
weaving and snaring and wounding all.

GUIDE

On the meed
 of His Yea
  I feed.
On the rock
 of His Nay
  I walk.

GOD'S ANSWER TO A PSALMIST

I had been lonely overlong,
Man, when I discovered you.
I was a lover choked with song
and with no one to sing it to.

A Juggler with no audience
doing my round of empty halls
I longed for one, wide-eyed, intense
to watch my myriad colored balls,

even a child to cup his chin
and wonder at my brilliant play,
at how I made the planets spin,
and tossed the sun to light his day.

So, 'What is man,' your psalmist cries,
'That I am mindful of Him?' Man?
He is that other pair of eyes
I've waited for since time began.

And when I plucked his shining face
out of the shadow of my mind
and shaped him forth from that dark place,
there was my joy at last defined.

W. W. E. Ross

THREE SPIRITUAL SONNETS

On the Supernatural

We must affirm the supernatural
However doubtfully we have looked upon
Its bare existence in the time that's gone,
For it is ever near and ever real;
As we shall find. We love the natural.
The human reason seated on a throne,
Creator of kingdoms for itself alone,
Is conscious of no zone ethereal.
But to an end with all this lower view,
The cause illusory, vain and yet employed; —
Angels there are and kindly daemons too,
Their throng, removed from faulty human sight,
In the unseen worlds as we should know in spite
Of natural explanation thin and void.

The Stream of Life

Angelic figures gliding in the stream
Of life, with a celestial sky above,
Show forth, embody the great rule of love
There underneath the illuminating beam
That through this spiritual zone doth gleam,
Making, itself, those mobile natures move —
Though none against the benign current strove —
Through the bright regions where fair spirits teem;
Where all is life and motion that employs
The energies ever of the creative light
That gleams and shows each heavenly nature young, —
The living light, mild, active, in the night
Even, of earth, most steadily fills with joys
Minds where a lasting melody is sung.

On Angels

Angels, as well as birds, on silent wing
Proceeding through the upper, open air,
Under the full intense celestial glare,
Perceive the true form of each earthly thing;
Birdlike the eye they deftly, subtly fling
Into the distance. Steadily they stare
Unhindered by the circumambient glare, —
Angels as well as birds can sweetly sing.
They too are known to hover above a nest
Wherein the swathéd soul of man doth lie
Soft-hidden deep in matter as in wool,
And theirs, too, the prerogative of rest, —
To soothe at times in manner wonderful,
With kind and piercing glance of soul and eye.

MARTYRS

Saints who were
slaughtered by
wild beasts in
blood-thirsty
Roman
arenas

gasping on
sand that was
red with the
blood of
martyrs

dying looked
upward to
where they had
seen a new
vision of
ecstasy

dying
received a first
glimpse of the
world
celestial.

THE RETURNING

Here, by the Christmas hearth, the heart remembers
　The loved ones, now no longer in the flesh,
Who shared with us the joys of far Decembers,
　Whose glances, in the fancy, shine afresh.

Their shadowy forms surround us in our musing;
　Their unseen hands upon our shoulders rest;
The sense of their affection comes suffusing
　The unforgotten anguish of the breast.

I see their dim, familiar faces smiling
　Upon our children whom they never knew,
Thus by their benediction reconciling
　The years that flow between us as they do.

It may be to their eyes' untroubled dreaming
　The youthful figures yonder are our own
As once we were, there in the firelight seeming
　Unchanging effigies from days now flown.

But no, these presences are not unwitting,
　In the high realm of their ongoing life,
Of all that passes with the ceaseless flitting
　Of time in our low world of finite strife.

We cannot see them, but their eyes are on us;
　We cannot touch them, but they touch us still;
Through joy and sorrow their deep glances con us;
　They watch our lives in love through good and ill.

Are these the spirits who have shared our living?
　Then still more close must be the Heart of Love
That in the climax of Creation's giving
　Came as a Babe, in pity from above,

The birth of God Himself in human fashion
    Hallows this season beyond word or thought,
For in His Birth we also see His Passion
    And an Atonement for his loved ones wrought.

And so enfolding all the glad endeavour
    In which, with the departed, we take part,
We feel God's living presence bless forever
    The peace of Christmas to the human heart.

F. R. Scott

ST. PETER'S

Out of the great doors flowed the appealing steps
Like a tongue of love, sucking me in.
I had travelled far. It was easy to say yes.

The huge interior opened fearful depths.
I crawled into the caverns and was lost.
The infinite spaces made me crave a guide.

But as the black frocks rushed to shepherd me
One lonely woman knelt down on bare stone
And the whole vast ruin shrank to marble paint.

Before any tree grew
On the ground,
Or clip of bird wing
Made sound,

Before cool fish drove
Under wave,
Or any cave-man
Made cave,

The clean aimless worlds
Spun true and blind
Unseen and undisturbed
By mind,

Till some expanding molecule
Of odd construction
Learned the original sin
Of reproduction,

Troubling the constant flow
With new activity,
Something beyond the grave
And more than gravity.

And so in shallow bays
And warm mud
Began the long tale
Of bone and blood.

The tale of man alive
And loth to die,
Of mine and thine and ours,
And the question, Why?

This was the turn of the tide,
The fall from heaven,
The spear in the side of God,
And time's division.

UNISON

What is it makes a church so like a poem?
The inner silence -- spaces between words?

The ancient pews set out in rhyming rows
Where old men sit and lovers are so still?

Or something just beyond that can't be seen,
Yet seems to move if we should look away?

It is not in the choir and the priest.
It is the empty church has most to say.

It cannot be the structure of the stone.
Sometimes mute buildings rise above a church.

Nor is it just the reason it was built.
Often it does not speak to us at all.

Men have done murders here as in a street,
And blinded men have smashed a holy place.

Men will walk by a church and never know
What lies within, as men will scorn a book.

Then surely it is not the church itself
That makes a church so very like a poem,

But only that unfolding of the heart
That lifts us upward in a blaze of light

And turns a nave of stone or page of words
To Holy, Holy, Holy without end.

LAST RITES

Within his tent of pain and oxygen
This man is dying; grave, he mutters prayers,
Stares at the bedside altar through the screens,
Lies still for invocation and for hands.
Priest takes his symbols from a leather bag.
Surplice and stole, the pyx and marks of faith,
And makes a chancel in the ether air.
Nurse too is minister. Tall cylinders,
Her altar-boys, press out rich draughts for lungs
The fluid slowly fills. The trick device
Keeps the worn heart from failing, and bright dials
Flicker their needles as the pressures change,
Like eyelids on his eyes. Priest moves in peace,
Part of his other world. Nurse prays with skills,
Serving her Lord with rites and acts of love.
Both acolytes are uniformed in white
And wear a holy look, for both are near
The very point and purpose of their art.
Nurse is precise and careful. She will fail
In the end, and lose her battle. Death will block
The channels of her aid, and brush aside
All her exact inventions, leaving priest
Triumphant on his ground. But nurse will stare
This evil in the face, will not accept,
Will come with stranger and more cunning tools
To other bedsides, adding skill to skill,
Till death is driven slowly farther back.
How far? She does not ask.
                              Priest does not fight.
He lives through death and death is proof of him.
In the perpetual, unanswerable why
Are born the symbol and the sacrifice.
The warring creeds run past the boundary
And stake their claims to heaven; science drives
The boundary back, and claims the living land,
A revelation growing, piece by piece,
Wonder and mystery as true as God.

And I who watch this rightness and these rites,
I see my father in the dying man,
I am his son who dwells upon the earth,
There is a holy spirit in this room,
And straight toward me from both sides of time
Endless the known and unknown roadways run.

Robert Finch

NOWELL, NOWELL

Once more fictitious joy is spread
In a display of green and red,
In paper bell that never rang
And holly wreath that never sprang
Brave from a snowy bed.

The family drift late to church
Leaving the housewife in the lurch
To tend her kitchen and prepare
The inevitable festal fare,
Menu of far research,

Sauces to blend and bird to baste
To tempt the individual taste,
The board must groan but not the guest.
The housewife does her level best,
Her critics do the rest.

Then presents will be swapped about
Each in a tissue paper clout
Which like the love upon the tag
Is dropt in the waste paper bag
Once the feared gift is out.

Children though asking for the whip
Receive instead the comic strip,
Their Christmas Day is mainly candy,
Toys, eats, the kicking up of shindy,
The movies and the pip.

Incessantly the doorbell goes,
The busy rush, the glutted doze,
And when the radio has hurled
In Christmas greetings from the world
The telephone will buzz.

The telephone, the radio,
If these were gone would Christmas go?
Can Christmas have been Christmas when
Peace on the earth good will to men
Was spread without those two?

What if some Christmas we were led
To leave untouched the green and red
The paper bell, the painted wreath,
The tissue love and what's beneath,
And greetings all unsaid,

And in the unaccustomed hush
Hear the celestial angel brush
The night apart, and dayspring tell
The coming of Emmanuel,
The quenchless burning bush?

THE ANSWER

One believes only what he understands?
The seasons smile from snow to summerhood
That their encored quartette is understood
And seeds applaud with tiny hidden hands.

One understands only what he believes?
But one believes that nations fail to learn
From old mistakes. The past is prologue? Turn
To this the sequel and explain our slaves.

One believes only what he understands?
If science be music, music science, the
Historian artist, art a history,
Where is the line drawn and who sets its bounds?

One understands only what he believes
To be congenial to his mental nature?
Though Buchenwald be credible, the creature
Iago is a fiction that deceives?

One believes only what he understands?
The fluctuating currents of affection?
The underlying ocean of reflection?
The wordless query suffering propounds?

One understands only what he believes?
But which comes first, belief or understanding?
Is love the recompense of comprehending
Or comprehension prize of him who loves?

One believes only what he understands?
Hoping a light, into the dark we go,
Hands must be clapsed before acquaintance grow,
The heart receives before the mind demands.

One understands only what he believes?
Belief is not exclusive to the mind,
Nor understanding, both belong in kind
To heart and soul, the three have strength that gives

Both more belief to what one understands,
More understanding to what one believes;
Commands of God can light to where he lives
The moment fear of God lights his commands.

If there be nothing that one can believe
The alcohol of self-belief is doomed,
The rouge of self-esteem and the assumed
Necessity for living, letting live.

If nothing is one cannot understand
Then what a world of Solomons we are
Unconsciously, securely unaware
That not our alleys but ourselves are blind.

Supposing one believed and understood
The whole. With no love, faith and understanding,
Though they move mountains, must at last have ending,
Spent by their spending, bodies without blood.

Love is belief and love is understanding,
Love looks and sees, love catches on and clings,
Love is not absent-minded, bears all things,
Believes all things, hopes and endures their minting.

Love is of God for God alone is love
And what he gives we give to him again;
His rain falls on the just and unjust, then
Returns to heaven but cannot stay above,

And Love Incarnate did come down like rain
On the dry soil of man's heart, mind and soul,
And rose again and still comes down for all.
Whoever turns to watch, or listens, fain,

Believes, and so, believing, understands
What is not understandable and ponders
The imponderable and wondering wonders
He used to wonder at what Love transcends,

Love, not a thing, a human yet divine,
One who fulfilled the law for those who fail,
The Pure who bore the impure past the pale
And died to turn our water into wine,

Who lives and moves yet not beyond our reach
For still he waits for those who toil to shore,
And on the fire of love Love's hands prepare
The meal of peace upon the peaceful beach.

THE THORN

They call me cruel thorn.
Thorn is my name,
Though none is ever torn
Because I aim.

Who made me cruel then?
The One who made me?
But I am fuel when
Greed or need need me.

They call me cruel thorn.
I, thorn by name,
Reddened when One was torn,
For the shame, not for shame.

When I as thorn shall cease
And, ceasing, free
Space for the fair fir trees
To follow me,

I'll cease, but not my praise.

THE ROOM

With these a room is made
For whatsoever guest:
An unprocrustean bed
For unbeclouded rest;

A table to provide
Converse and appetite
And, at his need beside,
A quiet place to write;

A stool, too, of a sort
Where he may sit and spell
The sayings of his heart
Or of Gamaliel;

Lastly, a candlestick
To hold a light for him
That no direction balk
And no intention dim.

O grant the grace to make
This room's equivalent
For others' and thy sake
And given, Lord, not lent,

Then bless what it is for
And whom, that so it might
Become the furniture
Of rest, love, learning, light.

THE EXEGETE

The sea of faith, you say. But faith is not
A sea because you say it is. The sea
Is set in bounds, faith has no boundary.
The sea moves like a clock, faith like a root.

The sea is faithful, faith cannot betray.
The sea's immune, faith cannot be betrayed.
The sea is fixed, of numbered droplets made,
Faith growing grows toward the perfect day.

The sea is universal, faith's unique.
Say that the heart's a sea and faith its moon,
Say that faith's moon is faithful to its Sun,
Say faith is strong though metaphor be weak.

A sea of faith? Faith little as a seed
Levels the sea of mountains doubt decreed.

THE HYMN

There is a sound exceeding art
When voices raise with true accord
The melody that in each heart
Comes from and seeks again the Word

For so it turns the night to day
Joining the song for inner ears
That the first singers of the Way
Led at the cross-roads of the years.

THE CERTAINTY

In the depths of the night I have heard, I know I have heard it
Clear and distinct from every sound by chance heard,
Unmistakable, for me, unmistakably worded,
In the depths of the night I have heard it and have answered.

As the stars were dissolving into the dawn I have smelt it,
Franker than sea-air, more pungent than sea-roses,
Something remembered before you have even felt it,
The breath of a flower one neither keeps nor loses.

At the height of the day I have seen, I say, I have seen it
More visible than anything else around it,
So visible that afterward where it had been it
Has left a more visible absence to expound it.

With the coming down of the twilight I have tasted
That which on tasting melted away like manna,
Leaving a hunger that ever since has quested
For hunger to hunger the better and the sooner.

Once in a timeless interim I touched it,
Alone in a crowd, crowding the other lonely,
Unheard, unseen, with nothing at all that vouched it,
I touched it, it touched me, once, once only.

HAS AND IS

Man is a body and he has a soul.
This you proclaim while all the world agrees,
And literature and art, if they would please,
Endorse your proclamation to the full.
Yet when the envelope with its address
And letter fade, the letter's words remain
Transformed to lasting notes of joy or pain
In the unfinished art of fugue we trace.
More than the alabaster is the ointment
Whose fragrance fills a house of many mansions,
Even more the hand that spills such sweet expansions,
Still more the heart that gives the hand appointment.
The sum of parts is less, here, than the whole.
Man has a body but he is a soul.

NOR ANY OTHER CREATURE

Bound opposite ways through a blizzard, they pass on the street.
One is old, one is young. They often worship together
But they meet in church as now they meet in the weather,
As contrary ages meet yet do not meet.

In church they sit at a distance, pray the same prayers,
Sing the same praise, share the same wine and bread,
Then leave to live the rest of the lives they lead
And to keep in order their separate affairs.

They may not again on earth come so close as today,
For while snow draws a curtain between them and wind lends wings
To their different errands, they share for a moment things
No parting will ever be able to take away.

These brothers in Christ, as they pass, both say hello,
Knowing they follow the same steps through the snow.

Louis Mackay

REND YOUR HEART AND NOT YOUR GARMENTS

Pity the innocent. There are none innocent, none.
Not all the quiet kindly men of good will.
We were weak who should have been strong, we were disunited,
We were smug, and lazy, and gullible, and short-sighted.
Whatever we did, there was more we should have done
Before there was nothing left to do but kill.

Now we squeal and squirm and shift and shuffle blame
On the paltry paladins that hold command
Because we let them. But God is not mocked.
Hell-gates are open; we could have kept them locked.
If it be shame to slay, on us the shame,
And if we die, we die by our own hand.

SONNET FOR MILITANT MORALISTS

GOD, who, at sundry times, in divers manners
Spake unto men, and was by men bespoken
To bless a quarrelling multitude of banners,
To break the proud, and pulverize the broken,
  GOD, by whatever name we think to name Him
For hallowing heroes when our mood is martial,
Whether we seek to claim, or to disclaim Him,
Remains most imperturbably impartial.
  We deem Him set above our clouds and clamour
Judge of Mankind, in Majesty resplendent,
Speaking clear truth through our disordered stammer —
But will He find for plaintiff, or defendant?
  We cannot answer; yet we think it odd
Our preference should bear no weight with GOD.

CAROL FOR 1938

O little town of Bethlehem,
How still we see thee lie;
Above thy dark and silent streets
The bombing planes go by.

O babes of Barcelona,
Children of far Chungking
To you what hideous anthems,
What herald angels sing

Of men set in high places,
In polite pretence
Slaying, and seeking out to slay
The holy Innocents.

Oh in how many hearts of men
Is kept the ghastly tryst
Where, on the grieving Christmas tree
Hangs crucified, the Christ.

Roy Daniells

PSALM 23

My enemies were certain I was starving,
It must have given them a fearful shock
Through the binoculars to see me carving
A roast of beef up on the barren rock.
And when I moved upon them down a byway,
Bathed and anointed, sweet with oil of rose,
They blanched for they had left me on the highway
Covered with blood and with a broken nose.
The landlord, in the arbour where I'm seated,
Has brimmed the bowl with wine, the bubbles wink.
It's time my gasping enemies were treated,
Do tell them to come in and have a drink.
And any day they like they may appear;
Thanks to the landlord, I'll be living here.

BROTHER LAWRENCE

He practised the presence of God. I do not know
Whether he moved to the divine mood or whether
God of his grace came where he was. Together
God and the ex-corporal made it so.
Not in some realm of transcendence but here below.
Here at his round of duties his small tight tether
Kept him. Only they sent him in bad weather
To buy wine for the brethren in Bordeaux,
Or was it Belfort?
                              Lawrence these centuries dead
Could he return would tell us how it was done,
Give us the formula for bringing power,
Love, joy into the weary head,
Give us the phrase that would call out the sun
And show the eternal springing in the hour.

THE WICKET GATE

Good solid Bunyan, but not sound at all
In this. How you reach the road it does not matter.
Bang on the wicket with a cry and a clatter,
Or if they shoot come scrambling over the wall,
Or wander in by a lane. If you have to, crawl
Out of a culvert so flat you can't be flatter,
Your clothes torn on the wire in one vast tatter.
Once on the road you're ready for the long haul.
Then in a sense you can relax, for here,
Strenuous as the going is, you'll end
By safe arrival. Look up, do not fear.
You have a guide, a comrade and a friend.
Though lions roar, though frightful giants appear,
Still waters and green grass are round the bend.

BALLAD OF KINGSTON

Take a morning walk in the elm tree park
Where the lovers have lain in the folded dark;
See the statue standing still and stark.
  Send me better men to work with
  And I will be a better man.

Don't look for an Apollonian grace
Nor yet for Caesar in his face
But read the legend on the base,
  "Send me better men to work with
  And I will be a better man."

As the good historian used to say,
We owe a great deal to old John A.
But he still was made of Canadian clay.
  Send me better men to work with
  And I will be a better man.

Damned compromise in everything,
From Mazarin to Mackenzie King,
And that's why the bells will never ring.
  Send me better men to work with
  And I will be a better man.

In Ottawa, that place of snow,
The palms and the laurels will not grow
And Lampman lies in the grave below.
  Send me better men to work with
  And I will be a better man.

If you wait for better men to come
You may wait for a century and then some,
To the end of time and the verge of doom.
  Send me better men to work with
  And I will be a better man.

When Christ by the sea of Galilee
Called out to the sons of Zebedee
They were men the same as you and me.
  (Send me better men to work with
  And I will be a better man.)

He gave them wine and gave them bread,
He gave them power to raise the dead,
And these are the words he never said:
  "Send me better men to work with
  And I will be a better Man."

ADESTE FIDELES

In neither joy nor triumph do I come,
Nor yet among the faithful, I'm afraid.
Somehow I must have missed the cavalcade;
The night is dark; I'm a long way from home.
The benefit of clergy, whether Rome,
Byzantium or Canterbury laid
Its hands, has never quite come to my aid.
I grope and stumble in the circling gloom
Circuitous and foiled.
                    Not lost, however!
An intermittent gleam breaks from the hill.
A strong invisible hand lays hold of mine
Even at the instant. My confused endeavour
Moves toward the height where I can see it still,
Sure that its shifting flame will shine for ever.

A. J. M. Smith

THE BIRD

Breast-bone and ribs enmesh
A bird in a cage,
Covered for the night with flesh
To still his vocal rage,

Curb his wild ardour and
Circumscribe his wing
Till One shall unwind the band
And let the door swing.

Free then of the flesh hood
And the cage of bone,
Singing at last a good
Song, I shall be gone

Into that far and wild
Where once I sang
Before the flesh beguiled,
And the trap was sprung.

GOOD FRIDAY

This day upon the bitter tree
Died one who had he willed
Could have dried up the wide sea
  And the wind stilled,

And when at the ninth hour
He surrendered the ghost
His face was a faded flower,
  Drooping and lost.

Who then was not afraid?
Targeted, heart and eye,
Struck, as with darts, by godhead
  In human agony.

For him, who with a cry
Could shatter if he willed
The sea and earth and sky
  And them re-build,

Who chose amid the tumult
Of the darkening sky
A chivalry more difficult —
  As man to die,

What answering meed of love
Can this frail flesh return
That is not all unworthy of
  The god I mourn?

CALVARY

A gentle haggard countenance
Under black thorns putty-pale
Has hushed the planets' morris dance
And rent the temple veil
And flung the moving lance
Of a world-destroying gale.

BESIDE ONE DEAD

This is the sheath,
  the sword drawn,
These are the lips,
  the word spoken.
This is Calvary
  toward dawn;
And this is the
  third-day token —
The opened tomb
  and the Lord gone:
Something whole
  that was broken.

Alfred Bailey

SEED

entangle me o lord in thy meshes
that I may rest in air
when water needs nothing.
look down, look down
where the green weeds move
in the flooding tide.

entangle me in the wind
let me sever, and sow
plants in the meadow
by the hill stream

the lord is my shepherd
I shall not want
the tips of the fingers
the roots of the trees.

TRUMP

and so I will write down
what I must
or go to wordless fields of stuff
beyond the nones
cradled in the great stare
unrocked   uncomforted
so I will if I can
I will write away the   emptiness,
make a firmament of words
the Word
name pain, invoke an ark
become
if to utter is to live
this will I do, and
        give if I can
        and give.

TRIAL AND ERROR

The earth's sick voices may be silent soon,
and one affair with Matter be enough.
A providential tear (with accent gruff
evoked by ailing creatures' plaintive croon)
might fall like rain upon a downcast moon
whose light went out at having called the bluff.
The Logos, having posed as such, might puff
the Flesh away it fed with tender spoon.
If this should happen, would He store the sea
against another day of pain and ache?
(revive a memory of the cosmic face?)
or spill it in a void and, shaking free
from His own imperfection, sadly take
His way beyond the wreck of time and space?

WORDS FOR A RESURRECTION

Each pale Christ stirring underground
Splits the brown casket of its root,
Wherefrom the rousing soil upthrusts
A narrow, pointed shoot,

And bones long quiet under frost
Rejoice as bells precipitate
The loud, ecstatic sundering,
The hour inviolate.

This Man of April walks again —
Such marvel does the time allow —
With laughter in His blessèd bones,
And lilies on His brow.

SOLILOQUY FOR BELLS

Bells in this steeple drip with sound
 When ushering a bride;
And dully toll with clumsy tongues
 When man or maid is dead.
For souls new-sprung and laved in grace
 They fling ecstatic peals;
Announce each novice to the font
 In liquid syllables.
They stammer through the Angelus;
 Drowse out the Vesper note;
Flute Matins thinly; sigh and swoon
 When Christ is lifted up.

J. M. Cameron

THE LYDIAN STONE

Lydian stone. A black variety of jasper used by jewellers
as a touchstone for testing gold.

For love or friendship requisite,
In dialectic apposite,
Take no pilgrimage without one,
Comforting to have about one
In the winter of our dearth.
Dragon-seed and sacred earth
Are the copulative pair
Raging in the golden air
Whence the descending Lydian stone
Draws its virtue.
                        Set upon
A field of gold it keeps its jet,
Kissing pinchbeck it will sweat
A scornful dew and milky stains
Mark the appearing Lydian veins.

Now if the dark betray the gold,
Old rags the silk and flame the cold,
The dark's a tutor, flame a school,
And old rags by negation rule.
The crooked wall defines the straight,
The unbroken hedge predicts the gate,
And even sins may purchase bliss.

I, a sinner, tell you this.

The storks come every year the crows
tumble   paper in the wind
always the imploring twilight
tortures us with its argument   stars
provide an idea of what is always
always always   but men die
and rot down to the bone   and grin

Your cheek is firm   your eyes
are fiery opals   your mouth is
sugar and spice more than the others
your tongue is music   your throat
beats a soft drum   your hand
this spiders in blue
the fortunes of love its maze and city

Famous Pythagoras   Plato
made all your bodily passions
badges of a consuming fever
and the flesh will peel   the bones
will show through falling flesh   the tongue
throat   hand   eye fall into the earth
and all shall be geometry   You could never dream

of what is prepared what is impossible
always and always   that the sound
the universal sound should crack
death's cold torpor   decreeing concord
between bone and dust   a marriage
of passions and organs   eyes glowing
sweet mouth   sweet music   love's city in your hand

Three move to the kill:
One to slay and eat
One to publish the death
One to hold the dish.
This of all dying is sweet
And sweet under the lash
And sweet upon the stone
And sweeter to the tooth
Than silver to the bell
Across the evening sun.

Hidden within the cloud
Of his accomplices
The one who slays cries out
The riddle of the stone:
Taken upon the road,
Torch-glare, embraces,
Delivered and undone,
To the court, by the lover;
So strange a gift is bought
Once, and for ever.

Heavy within a book
The hieroglyphs of guilt
Are dull upon the ear.
It is the killer's cry
Announces the assault,
Claws at the bowels, the air
Thickens, eyes burn, the tongue
Commands the spurt of joy,
Fountain, fire, song.

Killers have all the luck.

Over the fields with their strict rime,
The stiff hedge, the farouche hawthorn,
The mice come, the pastor with his pipe,
Ox, ass, goat, hare, coneys.

And the great owl, the mister facing-both-ways,
The disciplinarian, her bird after all,
Obsequious angel with white wings sailing
The sky raining down wisdom, the star

Splashing its milk on the frozen stone.
The hinge of the year groans. A child is wailing.
What particles of horse, of cat, what pollens,

What motes, what spores, what common effluvia

Excite him?
He cries no more. He is heaven-resolute
Cueillir dès aujourdhuy les roses de la vie.

Wilfred Watson

CANTICLE OF DARKNESS

I

Remind you, that there was darkness in my heart
And into the darkness in my heart
Sang light, and the singing light
Comprehended the darkness, but the darkness —
How could the darkness comprehend
The singing light ringing in my heart?
Which was not peace but storm, the gull
Flying, and the water pouring its wave
Into the wind's teeth, and the gull
Crying into the mouth of the harbour
Which was not peace but the sea's jaw

II

Know you, that all knowing must sing again
In the love which sang, the first light commanded,
The waters divided, the earth parcelled out
For flowers, beasts and creeping things,
The air given for birds,
The sun made round and warm,
The moon mild as milk — but how can I begin?
For the singing light was wrath not peace —
O Venus, your love was the sea's jaw

III

Best you, might we not lie sleeping in the dark
Of darkness, in the nothing which is our womb?
Lie sleeping, and never cough at the air?
Lie sleeping soft, folded up quiet and warm?
And never suckle the teats of despair?
Does not the singing light, sing us into the storm,
Light us to the tomb? O Mary, the door
Of our home, O let the night cover
The light which is our doom

IV

Stand gentle in my words. It was
The Friday of roses. And there was a rose
Singing the red song of your blossom.
When I came to the rose, there was
Gethsemane. When I came to Gethsemane
There was the rose. Stand gentle in my words
It was the Friday of Golgotha, the place
Of skull. O cross of petals —
O crossed petals —
Stand gentle in my words. For I thought
It was the rose of crucifixion, till I knew
It was the rose of resurrection. Stand
Gentle in my words. Saying I saw

V

The things of the world drop their skins.
Saying I saw white wings swanning in
Endless flocks of white. Saying I saw
The earth like a white lamb walking
Beside the mother ewe. Saying I heard
The nations like a lost calf bawling
For the mud flanks of the cow. Stand
Gentle in my words. I saw the darkness
Tremble. I heard the darkness singing.

VI

Tell you, darkness was pierced by the rose
Which vanished in a sun. Tell you, it was
A sun of glory the singing rose was
Saying. From the rose to the woman.
From the woman to the man. From the man
To the sun. From the sun to the earth,
Beasts, and all creeping things. To the waters
Divided. To the light created. And the singing
Rose sang in the lap of Mary. Darkness
Sang to the light and the kiss of love was peace.

THERE IS NO PENANCE DUE TO INNOCENCE / DECONSTRUCTED

```
                    1   bodies,
                    1   village,
        blasted;    2
                    2   tribal,
                    3   after
            of;     3
                            the   4   bombfall;
                                  4   the
                    5
        global      5   village
                                  6   Peace
                            of.   6
            on,     7   in,
        flowers,    7   flowers
                                  8   the
                            be    8   unto
9   earth
9   you
        the rose    1   isn't,
                    1   o rose
                    2   love, kids, mankind,
            of      2   lima
    isn't, aren't   3
            o       3   rose
                          rose,   4   kids, love,
                                  4   of
mankind isn't,      5   aren't
        lima        5   pray
                        mankind,  6   love, kids,
                            for   6   us
            rose    7
                    7   rose
                          pray    8   for
                            of    8   lima
9   us
9
```

Kay Smith

I CRADLE A STONE IN MY HAND

I cradle a stone in my hand.
A black stone, shining wet and smooth as the flank of a wave,
Shaped and grained by wind and tide.
How many aeons have brought it to perfection?
I rejoice in its being at home in the universe
And in the wholeness of its being.
Who would think a stone could nourish a dream,
Its cool curve like a phrase completing a poem?
How long, O Lord, how long before we know
In ourselves and our world
The full flowering of the human?

CHOICE

Time seemed to impose a choice:
Standing to water the plants
Or kneeling to say her prayers.
She stood to water the plants
And discovered the act was the prayer.

The day blossomed as roots drank deep.

A great poem
leaves a silence
heard after a mountainous wave
has broken.

In the dream, in the charmed dream we are flying
not as a kite held at the other end by hand of flesh,
rich in the smell of grass and colts munching
in the sunned field and air smooth as milk,
but with the limbs and torso webbed with a metal boldness,
scorning the matters of earth, the mole, the blind mole's wisdom,
bodies under the tree and a sweetness clouding the tongue.

In the dream, in the charmed dream, we alone have motion,
the world below a still life bathed in a green pre-thunder light,
hand on the wheel stuck like a fly in syrup,
the shovel raised never to fall, eyelid staid as a stone.

In the awakening, in the crash of awakening,
the heart is jolted into its eye,
the ancient oak in the dream an acorn
crowds into the eye,
the seed of Adam enters, Man of Sorrows,
with the eternal stars of wounds in His thigh;
in the dream, in the charmed dream we were flying
out of mind, who now are grounded with the slow root
in the invaded womb of time.

A VOICE THAT IS NOT A VOICE

I try to speak to God
but my thoughts
will not settle
the feathery seeds
of a
five O'clock
are carried away
at the nudging of a finger

Through the open window
I hear a child calling out something
on the edge of a wind
green
with leaves flowing into it
on a dark morning
before rain

Suddenly
the words of the child that I cannot reach
as they fly with the wind
leave behind
a pool of
greenness
out of the wind
and when I look into it a voice that is not
a voice
opens in me

George Johnston

THE OLD MAN

It serves the old man right,
Right is what it serves him,
Coming out in the light,
  Out of his leafy dark,
If life's glare unnerves him.

Now he is cross and blind,
Light has left him blinded,
He gropes about to find
  The dark he came out of,
But all darks are minded.

I know the poor old man,
Know him in my small heart;
I shun him when I can.
  Who chose for him? I ask.
His part is not my part.

Nevertheless I see
Him everywhere I look,
In me or out of me,
  His hunting, dazzled eyes
Give me back my own look.

Christ have mercy on me,
Forgive this mortal fear;
My five wits have drawn me
  Out, into the open,
And only you are near.

NO WAY OUT

No excuse
  Though I keep looking for one;
No use
  Pretending it is not me, has not been done.

No way out
  But always further in
In doubt,
  Fate-strong, heart-struck, wearied by sin.

I have not
  Seen Paradise, nor its trees,
But what
  I glimpse of unspoiled brings me to my knees.

THE BLESSED ANGEL

A blessed angel lighted at my window
  — One of those I knew when I was born —
And, with his big wings fanning the air inward,
Studied me, but otherwise no motion.

It was a dark afternoon, I remember the clouds
And a noise among the fields, empty and loud;
A noise in my own room, among the pictures,
And in the eyes of the angel angel pity.

His careless glory overwhelmed the room.
How kindly had he come! he broke my weakness
And, in his kindness, patted all my pieces,
Then off again to his tiny heaven flapped.

LAURA'S FUNERAL

for Aileen

Much gets remembered: the good
she did; how she did it,
as though, What else but do good?
Small things too, the tilt
of her gait and smile,
a way she had of turning up
without warning.
That was her way of going.

At her funeral
it welled up and brimmed over.
Then her priest tells a story
that brings back
her all but presence.

A life takes on its meaning
at the end, however sad,
however unbearable.
Dear God, dear dead, it gets borne.

DAISIES

Stars
in a pastoral heaven;

eyes
with a queen's look;

fiat mihi
in petals;

Mary's flowers
bosomed among the grasses.

George Whalley

LAZARUS

A simple command cuts his death to the bone.
A stiff shadow, bound, moves out of the cave
Blurred in drifting clouds of recognition.
Dappled with hot shadow of olive-leaves,
Gnarled with the ancient anguish of the vine,
He stood stone-still, carved out of the indrawn
Breath of morning, shriven, his neck arched back
Like a frozen wave. Only the women move,
Mary and Martha rocking to and fro
Like bladderwrack in an indolent undertow.
"Come home from the dead, Lazarus" —
The women had keened away the three nights
Never dreaming their salt and hopeless grief
Could turn their prayer to bitter affirmation.

Over the vibrant silver of the olivetrees,
Across the vine-plants and shadow, the day
Had curled in an arch of lapis lazuli.
Crisp with menace and dawning voices,
The plumed sunlight coils its force and strikes
A hammer-blow full on the creased eyelids,
On eyeballs wrinkled by the gravebands, bruised
By the brass pennies. Miraculous, the light
Breaks open his eyes as though his skull had split
On some relentless reef of lamentation.
His head strains back, arching his neck to the impact.
The hush of harvest on the taut skins of his ears,
The memorable feel of his own body
Bound still, the animal moanings of the women
Insistent as the fricture of cicadas —
Out of this undertow he claws his way
To a bitter beach of consciousness.

His eyes, unshrouded now, are windows looking
Inward and outward. No eye dare meet them.
Even the women edge their shame away
Disavowing their knowledge and their prayer.

The shrivelled heart may know
The royal reprieve of greenness.
But what imperial purpose,
Infinitely gentle,
Requires this hard penance
Fathering an old crime
On new innocence?

The stiff spasms of his waking overset
The calculus of grief and the cold
Merciful mechanism of forgetting.
His body's musk and myrrh is tropical landfall,
Languid repose transfixed by arrows of regret.
Stricken by the two-edged sword of paradise,
His neck arched back, he raises stone eyes
To the blaze of a bitter vision — pity granting
Life, withholding heaven. Nevertheless
The fluttering hands of embalming sorrow
Quicken like flowers inward, enfold and cherish
A man-child, it may be, or the seeds of a woman's
Grief, or some more numbing, some more precious
Mystery nourished of suffering — perhaps
An alabaster box of spikenard.

For the sword was made flesh
And dwells among us.

Destroying that we be not destroyed,
following darkness into darkness
we know not what we do. Unhating,
we work through the passionless precision
of instruments: and leave in our wake
the silence of the great cities, the broken
quiet of those who go down to lipless
silence. What wounds we leave we know not,
what self-inflicted wounds we know not,
following darkness into darkness,
destroying that we be not destroyed.

Forgive us. For we know not what we do.

R. J. MacSween

THE HERETICS

if only the old heretics
would return
to frighten the new heretics
how they would glare around
like a master returned to his classroom
to find the children in disorder
what goes on here
he would bellow
don't you know
that disorder is a thing earned
how dare you usurp my place

can't you see one of them
his hair awry
lion eyes bull shoulders
who dares to elbow into his territory
of freedom and defiance

I faced kings and popes
torture ostracism death
so that I could place my feet
upon this windy stage
while the audience gapes in wonder
the crowd outside seethes
and in far-off cities
across the Alps
glass splinters on the floor
and cardinals whisper
behind their hands

I would like to see
the new heretics
think of the old heretics
and listen to them
hear in their minds their names

the name of Berengarius
like the mutter of thunder
rolling up the deep ravines
of the Atlantic coast

PAIN SHALL BE NO MORE

pain shall be no more
when that day shall be
I shall be no more

the bird beside the spring
drinks the clear water
some of it falls like blood
upon the green stones

then the bird sings
the flowers awake like stars
the gentle cress
bends in the quiet water

when pain shall be no more
these shall be no more
there shall be no flowers no leaves
no piercing song to the heart

when pain shall be no more
God's love alone will brood
above the stones earth's children
sucked clean by the loving sun

and the silence of God's reverie
will be the house of all that remains

the earth will listen stilly
for the song that has died away
its memory a dear echo
amid the empty caves

ARCTIC DAY

on this arctic day
  we thank God for warmth
especially for the body's chemistry
  sending hot blood to the cheeks
  color to the lips

the body stirs in its grave
  at the touch of the pale sun
  its distant brother
the sun flings itself forward
  on its journey through space
  to warm our bones

through the vastness of æther
  the golden flood
  glances off planets
    and meteorites
  wastes itself in the darkness
   among the stars
   where cold reigns forever

as if God reached forth
  from the secrets of things
   to enfold to warm us
now we pulse in his hands
  like birds.

James Wreford

THE ANGEL IN THE WOOD

In nights of sin I hear
a rush of darkness near —
the angel of despair.

His wings like thick clouds are
that blot out every star,
obscure the map I bear

the tried geodesy
of reason, and the key
of Man's experience here

who daily wonders why
between the earth and sky
morning can be so fair

and evening in the wood
can fire the slowest blood
singeing the crimson air.

But O, though I withstood
the angel in the wood,
there is a fury there

not faith nor weeping may
nor all my fierce essay
turn from me or repair —

this dark and wintry sky,
this angel that is I,
the fury of my fear.

From hearts hard as the ground
bleak as the wintry sky
still as the stilly ice
comes up the human cry.

We from our hunger call
for Heaven's sustaining grace:
but what should draw Heaven's love to earth
to save the mortal race?

Though we in blindness seek
His light to mend our loss:
what is there in our worthlessness
should bring Him to the cross?

What is there in our shame
our doubt, our disbelief
to bind His head with thorns
His heart with human grief?

And yet He loves and will
with an unswerving care
take on the cure of all our wrong
and all our sorrow bear.

O surely this is love,
not that we cry His name,
but that, unloved, He loved us still,
and still unloved, He came.

Heavenhold of heart hope
not beauty only or the great breaking-out-
from-the-cloud bright light
for us, but brute force of wordwork
and wielder of wit —
come, be our fierce, perhaps, but fine
felicity and find;
the asunder-under-us terror
of windwoe against wind,
free flash of thesis
against antithesis,
christcross both and childfold — Thou
Wordwit of God, come, Jesus.

Fred Cogswell

ALOYSIUS SULLIVAN

Each Sunday morning if the day was clear
Before St. Vincent's steps we'd get together
And talk about our crops and wonder whether
Potatoes would be cheap again this year.
Then boys from far would meet with girls from near
As mothers smiled and ceased to watch for danger
Because they knew quite well each handsome stranger
Could hardly be a Protestant, and here.

But when the Father came, into the pale
Strained light we'd step, and not a single noise
Except the Latin and the bell would come.
One by one we'd go before the altar rail
Like strangers in a lonely land, come home
To the one place where union needs no voice.

THE CROSS-GRAINED TREE

With axe and adze slow Joseph hewed the tree
And scowled to watch the way its cross-grain curled,
Nor dreamed such poor and knotty wood would be
A lathe on which his son would turn the world.

A SUNBEAM ROLLED THE STONE AWAY

A sunbeam rolled the stone away
From off the grave of murdered love,
And from these walls of bone and clay
There rose by miracle a dove.

It gave a little joyous cry
And flew, all light and free from pain:
Nor can I coax, for all I try
It back to death with me again.

A CHRISTMAS CAROL

The holly wreath that now
Our house adorns
Will wither soon and be
A jagged crown of thorns;

Nor when fir needles fall
Can tinsel hide
The grey and naked limbs
Of the tree crucified;

The fair feast of Christmas
Our flesh enthrones
Even as we gaze piles up
A hollow heap of bones;

By which I know a sad
And doleful thing
That though we eat and drink
And gladsome carols sing

The ancient curse still blights
The human tree
And things men touch become
Shadows of Calvary.

THE WEB: FOR EASTER

Our feet that danced on morning ways
slowed to a fumbling crawl
as one by one the outward rays
broke on a narrowing wall;

then as we searched beneath the eaves
of slanting light and cloud,
the web the greedy spinner weaves
closed round us like a shroud;

and when One came Who laughed at loss
and braved its inmost lair
where taut threads joined to form a cross,
the spider caught Him there;

but as in blood our hope decayed
out of His seeded heart
He, dying, grew a thin green blade
that thrust the web apart.

What if I choose
to talk to myself
by finger-touch
on coloured stones?

meanings that my hands
assign their shape and texture
recur more true
than any sound

and God whose stillness
speaks as loud as noise
will understand
my private prayer

and listen to that part
of me which dies
a dumb fish beached
on a sand of words

Margaret Avison

EASTER

Now that the eve of April brings
    A delicacy of light at the day's end
        The bulge of earth seems again comic, and,
            On it, the city sails along the swerve
                Into the depthless diapason, pink,
Absurd, queer as a chemist's liquid, cloudless,
    Then filmed, then wind-fomented
        And flashed and flung about with rivers of rain.

        After the blur of doves the milky air
        Lulls, and listens, and there
        Is the sorrow of all fullness.
But on the hillside the frail tremulo
    Of a new dayspring, eggshell and lilac, wanders
        through the drenched quiet branches.

A bird sings, forceful, glorious as a pipeorgan,
And the huge bustling girth of the whole world
Turns in an everywhere of sunwardness
Among the cloudcarved sundering of its oceans.

A STORY

Where *were* you then?
    At the beach.
With your crowd again.
Trailing around, open
to whatever's going. Which one's
calling for you tonight?
    Nobody.
I'm sorry I talk so. Young
is young. I ought to remember
and let you go and be glad.
    No. It's all right.
    I'd just sooner stay home.
You're not sick? did you
get too much sun? a crowd,
I never have liked it, safety in numbers
indeed!
    — He was alone.
Who was alone?
    The one
    out on the water, telling
    something. He sat in the boat that
    they shoved out for him, and told
    us things. We all just stood there
    about an hour. Nobody
    shoving. I couldn't see
    very clearly, but I listened
    the same as the rest.
What was it about?
    About a giant, sort of.
    No. No baby-book giant.
    But about a man. I think —
You *are* all right?
    Of course.
Then tell me
so I can follow. You all
standing there, getting up
out of the beach-towels and gathering
out of the cars, and the ones
half-dressed, not even caring —
    Yes. Because the ones
    who started to crowd around were

so still. You couldn't
help wondering. And it spread.
And then when I would have felt out of it
he got the boat, and I could
see the white, a little, and
hear him, word by word.
What did he tell the lot of you
to make you stand? Politics?
Preaching? You can't believe everything
they tell you, remember —
    No. More, well, a
    fable. Honestly, I —
I won't keep interrupting.
I'd really like you to tell.
Tell me. I won't say anything.
    It is a story. But
    only one man comes.
    Tall, sunburnt, coming
    not hurried, but as though
    there was so much power in reserve
    that walking all day and night
    would be lovelier than sleeping if
    sleeping meant missing it, easy
    and alive, and out there.
Where was it?
    On a kind of clamshell back.
    I mean country, like round about here,
    but his tallness, as he walked there
    made green and rock-gray and brown
    his floorway. And sky a brightness.
What was he doing? Just walking?
    No. Now it sounds strange
    but it wasn't, to hear.
    He was casting seed,
    only everywhere.
    On the roadway, out
    on the baldest stone,
    on the tussocky waste
    and in pockets of loam.
Seed? A farmer?
    A gardener rather
    but there was nothing
    like garden, mother.

Only the queer
dark way he went
and the star-shine of
the seed he spent.
(Seed you could see that way —)
In showers. His fingers
shed, like the gold
of blowing autumnal
woods in the wild.
He carried no wallet
or pouch or sack,
but clouds of birds followed
to buffet and peck
on the road. And the rock
sprouted new blades
and thistle and stalk
matted in, and the birds
ran threading the tall grasses
lush and fine
in the pockets of deep earth —
You mean, in time
he left, and you saw
this happen?
The hollow
air scalded with sun.
The first blades went sallow
and dried, and the one
who had walked, had only
the choked-weed patches
and a few thin files
of windily, sunnily
searching thirsty ones
for his garden
in all that place.
But they flowered, and shed
their strange heart's force
in that wondering wilderness —
Where is he now?
The gardener?
No. The storyteller
out on the water?
He is alone.

Perhaps a few
who beached the boat and
stayed, would know.

PERSON

Sheepfold and hill lie
under open sky.

This door that is "I AM"
seemed to seal my tomb
my ceilinged cell
(not enclosed earth, or hill)

there was no knob, or hinge.
A skied stonehenge
unroofed the prison?
and lo its walls uprising,
very stone drawing breath?

They closed again. Beneath
steel tiers, all walled, I lay
barred, every way.

"I am." The door
was flesh; was there.

No hinges swing, no latch
lifts. Nothing moves. But such
is love, the captive may
in blindness find the way:

In all his heaviness, he passes *through*.

So drenched with Being and created new
the flock is folded close, and free
to feed — His cropping clay, His earth —
and to the woolly, willing bunt-head, forth
shining, unseen, draws near
the Morning Star.

. . . PERSON, OR A HYMN ON AND TO THE HOLY GHOST

How should I find speech
to you, the self-effacing
whose other self was seen
alone by the only one,

to you whose self-knowing
is perfect, known to him,
seeing him only, loving
with him, yourself unseen?

Let the one you show me
ask you, for me,
you, all but lost in
the one in three,

to lead *my* self, effaced
in the known Light,
to be in him released
from facelessness,

so that where you
(unseen, unguessed, liable
to grievous hurt) would go
I may show him visible.

BRANCHES

The diseased elms are lashing
the hollowing vaults of air.
In movie-washroom-mirrors
wan selves, echoing, stare.

O Light that blinded Saul,
blacked out Damascus noon,
Toronto's whistling sunset has
a pale, disheartened shine.

If, like a squalling child
we struggled, craving, who
would hear wholeheartedness
and make the world come true?

In ancient date-palm-tasseled
summer, King David knew.
Thus seeds could continue splitting
and oceans rolling blue.

The cinnamon carnation
blows funeral incense here.
In darkness is a narcotic,
a last rite, silenced care.

Can *this* kind of blanking
bring us to our knees?
Christ, the soldiers blindfolded you
and slapped mouth and teeth

asking you "Who?"
and nothing was said.
You knew.
And knew they needed bread.

The elms, black-worked on green,
rich in the rich old day
signal wordlessness
plumed along the Dark's way.

Stray selves crowding for light
make light of the heart's gall
and, fly-by-night, would light on
the Light that blinded Saul.

But he died once only
and living bright, holy, now,
hanging the cherried heart of love
on this world's charring bough.

Wondering, one by one:
"Gather. Be glad."
We scatter to tell what the root
and where life is made.

WATER AND WORSHIP: AN OPEN-AIR SERVICE ON THE
GATINEAU RIVER

On the pathway mica glints.
Sun from the ripple-faceted water
shines, angled, to gray cliffs and the blue sky:
     from up here the boat-braided river is
     wind-riffled, fishes' meadows.
                  But at
          eye-level, on the dock, the water looks deep,
                cold, black, cedar-sharp.
          The water is self-gulping under
          clefts and pier posts.

We listen.
your all-creating stillness, shining Lord,
trembles on our unknowing
             yearning
                   yielding lives:

     currents within us course
     as from released snow, rock —
     sluiced, slow welling from
             unexpected hidden springs,
     waters still acid,
     metallic with old wrecks —
          but Love draws near,
          cut-glass glory, shattering everything
                        else in
          the one hope known:

     (how are You so
     at home with what we know?)

The waters lap.
Rocks contain and wait
in the strong sun.

        "Joyful, joyful, we adore Thee . . . . "

The word read by the living Word
sculptured its shaper's form.
What happens, means. The meanings are not blurred
by Flood — or fiery atom.

> He reads: a Jewish-Egyptian
> firstborn, not three years old;
> a coal-seared poet-statesman;
> an anointed twelve-year-old.

The Word dwells on this word
honing His heart's sword,
ready at knife-edge to declare
holiness, and come clear.

> Ancient names, eon-brittled eyes,
> within the word, open on mysteries:
> the estranged murderer, exiled, hears at last
> his kinsman's voice;
> the child, confidingly questioning, so close
> to the awful ritual knife,
> is stilled by another, looking to His Father —
> the saving one, not safe.

The Word alive cherishes all:
doves, lambs — or whale —
beyond old rites or emblem burial.
Grapes, bread, and fragrant oil:
all that means, is real
now, only as One wills.

> Yes, he was tempted to wash out
> in covenanting song
> the brand on the dry bone;
> he heard the tempter quote
> the texts he meant and went embodying.

> The Word was moved
> too vitally to be entombed
> in time. He has hewn out
> of it one crevice-gate.

His final silencing endured
has sealed the living word:
now therefore He is voiceful, to be heard,
free, and of all opening-out the Lord.

LISTENING

Because I know
the voice of the Word
is to be heard
I know I do not know
even my own cast burden,
or oh, the costly load
of knowing undisturbed.
There is a sword
enters with hearing. Lord
who chose being born to die
and died to bring alive
and live to judge
though all in mercy, hear
the word You utter
in me, because I know
the voice.

OUGHTINESS OUSTED

God (being good) has let me know
no good apart from Him.
He, knowing me, yet promised too
all good in His good time.

This light, shone in, wakened a hope
that lives in here-&-now —
strongly the wind in push and sweep
made fresh for all-things-new.

But o, how very soon a gloat
gulped joy: the kernel (whole)
I chaffed to merely *act* and *ought* —
"rightness" uncordial.

But Goodness broke in, as the sea
satins in shoreward sun
washing the clutter wide away:
all my inventeds gone.

The cumbering hungry
and the uncaring ill
become too many
try as we will.

Try on and on, still?
In fury, fly
out, smash shards? (And quail
at tomorrow's new supply,
and fail anew to find and smash the why?)

It is not hopeless.
One can crawling move
too there, still free to love
past use, where none survive.

And there is reason in
the hope that then can shine
when other hope is none.

From the namby-pams
of the cloaking faith I wear
deliver me. From the times
peculiar persons, particular people-swarms
seem, from me, unfamiliar —
O from the namby-pams that evade
the absolute Scrutiny
and evade healing, o deliver me.
Whatever I read or hear or see
only declares what is in me,
an ominous freight
hidden — and worse let out . . . .
But from an omnibus
contrition burying
the sting of shame, of naming it,
deliver.

And from the pride in having none —
'I'm like that' or 'leave me alone;
I'm a dog, I'll worry this bone':
deliver me.

ALL YOU NEED IS A SCREW-DRIVER!

Frustration finds no anodynes
as hours of darkness rise and fall;
the 'should have dones,' the 'could have beens'
have me in thrall.

Sleepless? from creativity
in me, the spoiler. (Ah — when corn,
wine, creatures, suns, all came to be,
seventh-day Joy was born!)

A diagram a plastic sac
of bolts and screws and little pegs
a box of sides and front and back
and, yes, four legs.

The picture all completed glows.
You need your own tools too? just one.
And as adrenaline now flows:
it WILL be done.

Right the first time! ? Well, 'up ↑ ' is down.
What has been joined can come asunder.
Reverse, rescrew: the process known,
now there's no blunder.

Empty box two, spread out the plan,
begin assembling with a song.
With so much practice now, how can
this one go wrong?

It could. It did. 'This one' had glue
as well as pegs and so on. Haste
made waste: again the wrong way to,
and bonded fast.

Another day another try?
Pervasive smell and flaking smear
of glue — and solvent. Let it dry
and call an engineer.

Well, I am more than construct. No
diagram lays out how, or can say who.
Spoiler and spoiled betimes? I anyhow
can yet be made anew.

KNOWN

After the crash we scan
passenger lists — eyes dart
along, down, till at last we can
relax: this horror was not to the heart.

An "act of God," that tidal wave
or flood — or the lightning-bolt
that caused this crash? We have
His word, yes. He has all, controlled.

Oh, but His eyes are on
the passenger-list too;
every mourning child tonight's well-known;
their dead He, nearest, knew.
In charge — and letting us be — but *not* apart:
for Him this horror is real, and to the heart.

Our horizons stop at those we know
so we can bear it;
His, not at what we know,
compassing our sheer-edge-of-nothing panic
and more; He though in peace and power, knows pain
for time and space, Whom these cannot contain.

Douglas Lochhead

CHRISTMAS IN AUGUST

You say it is Christmas
in August —
Neighbour, I agree
because
under this leaf
is a tomato,
and another
and see
there are promises.
And I'll go along
with that —
Christmas in August.

But if we look closer
Easter is in it too —
the stake, the vine,
the red blood in the fists
and the death —
in this August.

AT THE TOP

The Christ   all given
all giving . . .

who still stands in the treachery
of those same garden shadows?

is life like that one asks
        seeing the Christs die

seeing the day's evidence,
        hearing the cock crow echoing   still
through suburban gardens
        the smell of lilac
brings all to a halt
                for a moment
but there is the same hurt
the same movement of hands
        down falling   needing
birds to carry them as wings
        to prayer
                and eyes
wide enough
        for the green boreal
the lights leading from ice
        showing a cross
at the top.

a ride of devotions
down this glide of easter &
while slicing ham the knife slipped
bringing blood over the table
but out of it small sympathies
surrounded the thumb, bandages,
& where behind a lily grew far away
to a stone street, braying animals,
the occasional gasp of voices
in the sleepless crowd, here,
in this place all lips held prayers
the white ghostly miracles
were seen and withdrew
& what was said was so, &
returning to this shared time
& table I tried to tell all
but only the meat in my hands
made sense at dinner
at easter

X

a grin box day gone cold cloud down
PAST FINDING OUT THE GREATER MYSTERY
GREET GREET THE DAY LIFE GLORY

a suffering hand undoes a frown
THERE IS A SOUL A GRACE A GREATNESS
GREET GREET THE DAY LIFE GLORY

my kite wears now a wild Christ's face
THE UNWELCOME WIND SPELLS PAST O PAST
GREET GREET THE DAY'S GONE STORY

almost not quite the kite whips harder
ALMOST LOST THE SOUL AND PULLING CHRIST
GREET GREET THE NEW LIFE GLORY

DEAD GULL

What is it?

grey blue white and black
while the lake
throws up a small sea
and wind comes in
on beginning combers

the elements,
your elements,
conspire, dead gull

dead-set your body
is already eye-less,
the past of searching
gone, probably,
your inland gliding
to fields and dumps

dead gull on narrow strip
of beach, I mourn

dead gull
spreading my arms over you
they make a shadow
of flight

but with what sun
there is,
my body and arms
build a dissolving cross,
a black stain of mourning
over your hard place —

Elizabeth Brewster

SUPPOSITION

Just for a moment, suppose that it were true,
That miracles were possible, even for oneself,
That the Holy Dove might actually descend.
Suppose that the God present in the wafer,
Swallowed like a seed, might spread his branches out,
A flourishing tree, putting forth virtues like leaves
And graces like fruit; suppose our guardian angel
Truly stands by us with his upraised wings
To protect us against the crowned and cruel arch-demon,
The evil enchanter with his wicked wand
Who casts his spell over our souls, poor birds
Caught in an eternal trap.

       Suppose that we're upheld
By the endless murmurs of prayer rising in swelling waves,
Gathered from the lonely, lost places of all the world
And having their sources in forgotten centuries.
Suppose that the lost voices of dead saints,
Mixing like incense with our own petitions,
Float them more gently to the gates of heaven.

Suppose, just for a moment, that God is real,
That, at the heart of this world where beauty walks with terror,
Where goodness and treachery are so strangely mixed,
There is goodness that is not ugly and beauty that is not cruel,
And peace that is true beyond all understanding.

Suppose this much to be true, and build upon it,
And hope what seems like sand may turn to rock.

Lady, I come to light
A candle in your sight.
So frail this flame, like faith,
That wavers at a breath,
Yet scoops from darkest space
A place of light and peace.

Oh, frail this candle's flame,
Frail every human name,
And frail and delicate
The flesh that worms will eat;

Yet from your flesh was made
God, when he came to aid
With his divine nature
His lost and fallen creature.

You shielded in your arms
Heaven himself from harm,
And soothed his baby cries
With tender lullabies.

Children, to you we run.
Pray to your little son
Whom you so softly hold
To save us from the cold
Of our own bitterness
By means of his dear grace,
Who made the heaven and earth
But chose a human birth.

Honouring you, he chose
To honour us (his foes,
As we had else become
Who madly loved our doom)

And gave to flesh and blood
A glory not allowed
To spirits, though they flame
With an angelic name.

Your womb, the marriage bed
Where earth and heaven were wed,
Brings forth perpetually
Our life, even when we die.

Lady, my candle's light
Will die in the deep night.
Protect my soul's frail spark,
Wavering in the dark;
And all these others too,
Light with serener glow.
Pray for us, Lady, who
Have lit our lights for you.

POEM FOR THE YEAR OF FAITH

Faith is not less faith because it fluctuates,
Even in the presence of God,
And I think it must have been hard to believe
On the day of the Crucifixion.
I imagine the Man with a dark, plain face,
Dominated by the great nose, the brown eyes
Of an anonymous sufferer I once saw
In a movie of one of Hitler's Camps.
A little past his prime (as a man in his thirties would be then),
No wonder he stumbled under the wooden weight
Of the great cross. But would a God stumble?
His followers must have wondered.
Had Judas' kiss been needed
To show which of these men claimed to be God?

And his Mother standing there to watch the hanging,
A stout, greying woman in her fifties,
This good Jewish matron taken from her kitchen
And her concern for a neighbour's wedding or childbirth,
Could she be the Mother of Sorrows and of God
Whose "Yes" to the Sprit had brought God to the world?
Could doubting Thomas and denying Peter
And that other Mary
(Neurotic, or disreputable, or both)
From whom the devils had been cast,
And the handful of disciples who were always wrong,
Always clumsy, always being rebuked
And getting into disputes about who was greatest —
Could they see visions, perform miracles,
Be saints and martyrs, found the Church of Christ?
It seems, indeed, they could.

Well, but they saw the Christ transfigured,
Or raised from the dead and eating fish and honeycomb.
They touched their hands to the still open wounds.
But if they had wished to deny, even so,
Would they have been convinced?
Executioners bungle; men have escaped the hangman
(A while, anyhow) and lived to tell the tale.

Was their faith, in the long run, different from ours,
Who still struggle with this strange, this harsh, this gentle
Man who was either God, or mad, or a trickster,
But must be God?
His words tantalize the doubting ear:
  "I am the Way."
  "I am the Vine."
  "I am the Bread of Life."
  "I have overcome the world."
  "I and the Father are one."
  "Come unto me."
  "I am with you always."
  "I am Jesus, whom you persecute."

And indeed the Presence is still here,
Tangible (sometimes) as the wounds were to Thomas.
It is not surprising that we sometimes forget,
That the Presence sometimes withdraws and is remote.
Perhaps there were days later when Thomas wondered
If he had really touched and seen, or if his memory
Was maybe playing tricks.
All he could do then was to do
As we still must,
Remember there were other witnesses,
Remember that we saw, will see again,
And wait, and wait.

The church is half-barn, half-forest.
Rafters stretch
in dim light, remote and branchlike.
The congregation rustles in.

Good Friday. Rain outside.
Umbrellas are parked dripping.
Here is shelter.
The choir will sing the Messiah.
We wait in ritual expectation.

Above in the branching rafters
a rustle, a flit of wings.
A child points. Another lifts her eyes.
"It's a bird."
"What is it?"
"It's a starling."
"It's a bird." "A starling."

Eyes turn, eyes gaze upward.
Flitting through branches,
perching on beams of the barn
in the dusty light,
the bird flies,
the mystery.

Who knows where it comes from
or where it goes to,
the bird that flies into the banquet hall
and out again?
If anyone can tell us news
of that bird
and its whereabouts,
we shall gladly listen.

This present bird, the starling,
cannot get out.
It flies up against the East Window,
the remote portrait of — is it? — Christ
and back again to a convenient beam.
It does not know what to do next.

"How will they ever get it out?
It's up too high for ladders."

The choir files in.
If its members see the bird,
they pay no attention.

It is a long afternoon.
All we like sheep . . .
We watch the bird.
He is resigned.
He is resting,
maybe listening.

The sparrow hath found a house . . .
Even thine altar . . .

The cross . . .
Suffering . . .
Lift up your heads, O ye gates.

Let him loose.
Let the caged spirit free.
The bird flits distractedly
here and there.
He cannot find the way.

Why do the kings of the earth rage
and the people imagine a vain thing?

The young man kneels,
head bowed, his children beside him.

He is angry.
War angers him.
The Lord will arise . . .

Behold, I show you a mystery.
We shall not all sleep . . .
We are back with you, bird,
confused, confined,
beating against the image,
caught between rafters and window.

Never mind, bird.
It's raining outside.
What would you do out there?
Better in here, in the barn
under the branches,
sheltering with mankind,
sheltering in the brave chorus
of hallelujahs.

Startled by the applause
you fly about wildly.
Be patient, be patient,
they will try to let you out

unless you fall first
crumpled, beaten, crazed,
the broken victim
on the altar

with the other Victim.

EASTER SUNDAY, QUAKER MEETING

I sit in a Quaker meeting
this Easter afternoon.
There are eight of us
on varnished chairs around a varnished table.
It is so still
I hear my neighbour's stomach rumble.
Another neighbour
begins to fall asleep.
I sit and daydream
of being in your arms.

Through stiff white curtains
the blue sunshine pours.
In the scrolled faded carpet
blue flowers twist in intricate patterns.
My eyes are on the floor
unless I raise them
to the shelf where someone has placed a flower pot
containing one ivy leaf.

Can the awaited Holy Spirit
console me for your absence?
Perhaps so.
I could put my head down now
on the flat varnished table
and fall asleep.
Or I could weep tears
of anguish, longing, desire, anger
for God

Or maybe you.

YOU SAY

You say I'll write about anything
("Anything's grist to your mill,"
is the way you put it)

Not true, I say
(sensing an accusation)
though in fact I wish it were true

for everything
God knows
ought to be written about:

no experiences, emotions so secret
or so boring
as not to deserve words
to clothe them or make them naked.

All animals, plants, stones
speak somehow,
unfolding meaning
in fur or petals

a deaf-mute finger-touch.

If I could be a burr
I might not need a written language

but, struggling to be human,
I speak as well as I can,
would like to speak more clearly,

would like to stand on the roof tops
naked
shouting my words.

On the Day of Judgment,
so they say,
what is whispered in chambers
is to be trumpeted on street corners.

A poem is
a small day of judgment.

THIS ELASTIC MOMENT

Yes we are that too: we are everything who feel it.
Everything that has meaning has the same meaning as angels: these
hoverers and whirrers: occupied with us.
Men may be in the parkgrass sleeping: or be he who sits in his
shirtsleeves every blessed Sunday: rasping away at his child who
is catching some sunshine: from the sticky cloud hanging over the
Laura Secord factory; and teetering on the pales of the green
iron fence: higher up than the briary bushes.
I pass and make no sound: but the silver and whirr of my bicycle
going round: but must see them who don't see: get their fit, man
and child: let this elastic moment stretch out in me: till that
point where they are inside and invisible.
It is not to afterward eat a candy: picket that factory: nor to
go by again and see that rickety child on the fence.
When the band of the moment breaks there will come angelic
recurrence.

THE BROWN FAMILY

All round the Browns stretched forty acres of potatoes.
They lived like squatters in my father's little chicken-house
That grew to lean-tos and then to a whole shack-town where married
Browns
Slept God-knows-how hilled in the darkness all night long,
Mornings how rolled out to breakfast on the lawn
Sitting in crumbs and clover, their eyes still glozed over
With dufferish sleep, and all stuffing away like Eskimos.

Brown boys had greasy jeans and oilcloth school-bags made at home
And sneakers for quick escapes through orchard gates,
Tom had two left thumbs while Ted was tough and dumb, but there was
much
Of army sadness to the way all their heads got furry as muskrats by
March.
Well after meagre spells Fall was their full season when they dropped
Partridge, pheasant and squirrel — shooting as if they would never stop
As later they crazily shot up even the apple-trees at Caen.

Their sisters inevitably called Nellie or Lily were deliberately pale,
Silly incestuous little flirts whose frilly skirts were dirty
From every ditch in the county. On lonely country roads under the moon
Their sadness lit like incense their sweet ten-cent perfume.
But at hint of insult their cheeks took on fiery tints those summers
When they hired-out to cook. And their eyes often had that strange blue
look
Of the blue willow plates round a rich farmer's plate-rail.

'What I can touch and take up in these two hands,' said Mrs. Brown,
'Is what I trust!' Accordingly on the bashed piano and on the floor, dust
And rich potato-coloured light everywhere mingled: scraps, fronds,
gourds,

Teazle, fossils, hazel wands, turkey feathers and furs . . . goods
All lovingly hers tangled. And all could be taken up, stroked, cajoled
In the same manner as her Old Man: for Mr. Brown's heart was pure
glossy gold
By tender handling, of all that's drossy, slowly, suvendibly, rendered
down.

But as alike as Anna Pauker's brood so that it tears the heart to see
Was that last lot and will all Browns ever be,
Picking and pecking at life, scratching where something is cached.
What are they looking for? Not lots to eat or wear. Not lots in town.
Strangely, that same thing *we* want would satisfy a Brown —
Something of the sort God gives us every day
Something we can take up in our two hands and bear away.

from THE PLANNED WOODLOT TO THE FREEDOM
OF MRS. FIELD

I. *The Planned Woodlot*

The planned woodlot
where we are the only things that move:
("and since that day no bird flies over Glendalough"
    — the Wicklow man telling it all in the bar
  this comes again where no bird flies)
and we are trees, tourists,
                              an air of wonder prevails:
the voice that stills the waters
(that floats there Players and Sweet Afton soft)
that is the bird
the bird that never sings
the song getting lost, you and I
drifting through the planned woodlot.

II. *Into the Trees*

"dear woods I know them all . . .
                              the day
when I have to leave them my heart
will be very heavy." Ah yes, Claudine.
Above my head the porcupines steadily munching chips,
on the edge of Grogan's old clearing a deer
poised leaf and silent in the glades
as sound of paper (pencil on)
pages,   leaves falling,
through the grey-brown shapes of sound
& the imperceptible drawing back of the bow.

III. Going for Water

Then the only sound in the August clear
is Carmen Sim's pumphandle
              creaking thirst
and we are going for our share
and we are crossing the back line, worsted,
gravelly and lately corduroy,
and we are feeling smoother now satiny
slipping over the weathered log bridge
tinpail aswing in our two hands,
and our bare soles touch down to August
and the big Grayling swish under the bridge.
Smooth, clear, we laugh once over,
twinned hands divining that instant caught
when someone somewhere is Really Praying.

Robert Beum

A DOOR

Why do I believe?
Not because I see
every world deceive
or show worlds of Thee;

nor does hope of life
contradicting sense
kneel me with my wife
in a crossed silence;

the seven proofs lie
unused; high and still,
verse has made me cry
like Golgotha Hill;

and I question well;
but once, Thy Son came:
spring in winter, fall
in summer — His name

then was His being;
and I saw Him close
a door, and seeing
that, my knocking grows.

THE SOURCES

This wall, that bridge, the structure of lines
We build and rebuild thinking the years
May shiver against them and find there
As in wall and bridge the heart's model,
All precision, all generous blood —
Shining of sources, of the Masters
And their suns, girls, flowers, horses, whales.

The fire storms that cooled into a sun
Printed with sunflowers and horses
And whales and rides down morning and mind,
The little tributaries to air —
Warm with depending, gladly not free
In the independent cold, sometimes
On a lonely day we ride like gods

And ride out in sidereal time,
Nothing less, on its horses and whales,
And would ride to creation's outskirts,
To the least underpinnings, dark suns
In the darkness praised only by God.
You hidden girds and little wellsprings,
Shine in our staves: we ride to your praise.

HYMN FROM A BRIDGE

Even to this wired air comes morning,
unknown morning — color, cloud, and wind
as they will, cobalt and gold like this
ringing all the yes of heaven, yes
of the first morning, waking even
on this bridge the world of the first wide
burnish of water in sweet quiet

and still this light becomes that other,
light no clever chemical or lens
or cable will carry or impair
or ambition or analysis
bury: sunburst of destination,
the dullest, the least of us, at home
in the unreached home of the morning.

A PSALM FOR SUMMER

Morning spun without care
and still with buzzing,

idle sun making honey
in the air and the heart,

easy start of a day,
easy we go forgetting

our cunning, forgetting
every way but the way

to the fields of summer,
the honey of praise.

✢ 169

MADRIGAL

Waiting well,
Hours without side,
Time not pride,
Will be saved.

Mornings given
To morning light,
Time not pride,
Will be praised.

Eyes that mean
Their smile, trust
Like a bride's,
Will be seen.

Springs that open
Praise not known
Will be shown,
Will come green.

Michael Parr

THE MAN IN THE JUDAS TREE

The man in the judas tree,
who wears my clothes but is not me,
shall stay there till I set him free.

Through sunrise and the silver set
twice thirty psalms will not forget
how high he hangs for my sake yet.

I dread him in my sense of touch
as one who fills the mouth with ash,
but he who loves him nothing lacks,

will put his sins on me for love
as bitter son of man I live
though God and all his angels leave.

Shall he hang high and I go free
who wears my flesh but is not me,
my Christ of rags in the judas tree?

WHEN I WAS FIVE

When I was five and held the hand of God,
I knew the shapes of evil and of good
and let what star would shine elect to guide,
for I was holy in the heaven's guard.

And double five made ten my wicked sense,
leaping from lights of love to finer sins;
in making wars upon a poor man's sons
I ran from treaties in those bloody scenes.

I split my twenty years of love for love
with any Eve my Adam would not leave
and wept for mercy that my wits could live
longer than thirty virtues and a laugh.

And yet in love for long, I'm Mary's man,
and these elusive years at last are mine.

LOOK, LORD

Look, Lord, at this smooth round pebble,
it moves in my hand like a parable:

in shape and texture it's a miracle,
with it men built the town of Jericho;

speeding through air, singing in the skies,
it measured Goliath, cut him down to size;

became sainted, O this holy stone,
killing martyrs, put on pious stain;

made images and subways in the church,
spire of promise, key to arch

and in the ways of sorrows in the city
it paved a pilgrimage to pity.

But now in arcs of sun it skims on water,
watched by a child, to wash until it wither.

Robert Gibbs

OLD MAN WHELPLEY

You hadn't reached your ninetieth year
  or taken your third wife
  when I knew you best
  saintly in your white whiskers
  rocking on your verandah
  in Beulah Campground
  where whitewashed stones
  spelled out in black
  shouts of the redeemed seldom heard
  and a sign on the beach said
NO SUNDAY BATHING PERMITTED

Your blue eyes steadied behind their glasses
  as they took the seven-mile measure
         of the Reach
  and you spoke heretically to one
  you thought might understand
  not of retribution
  in or out of a mad God's hands
  but of restoration
  your breath crowded with hosannas
  as your eyes sang the words they saw
         far off
THE RESTORATION OF ALL THINGS

Even the devil? the boy couldn't help asking
Even the devil — you said

FOR A NEW SEASON

On this last of my holidays the coldest and brightest
a dazzle off dry snow off
scalloped-over snowshoe tracks
epiphany falls   like a too sharp look

at a false Florida waterfall to blot
it out   At the back of my yard
two last sunflowers bow their
seeded combs like twin bishop's

crooks   agreed on a lowly gospel
The thorn tree finelined   shadowless
alive with its design looks satisfied
at rest   keener barbed   A couple

of puffed-out linnets   red polls
rattle railside bushes   Smokes
rise   cotton out   and down
catching gusts from a day not

still enough to stand in
To measure its cold I must go out
pendulummed with my Christmas-new pedometer
blindered in wolf-fur   deeply honey-

combed in thermal drawers   I squeak
I drink icy air   I wiggle my nose
to mobilise its tip   I slit my eyes like
my cat's at watch in a sunbeam

I taste woodsmoke   spice of city winters
long gone and country too
Each step confirms the snow's
tough springiness   It catches all

shadows inside   and lets
nothing out but blindingness
I take breaths too deep for
singing   to make this holy day last

A SESTINA FOR AN EASTER CELEBRATION

How far did he come that prince
putting away his crown and royal glory?
How far he came and to what town
you know the story of his descent
Before he spoke and had worlds spinning
already a lionhearted lamb

In that stable was there a lamb
to bleat with fear at seeing a prince
lie so low? What spinning
spiders in corners webbed his glory?
Did even flies of unroyal descent
light on his face in David's town?

His cousin the baptist outside of town
was the first preacher to call him a lamb
foretelling his rise and his own descent
with all old ways And that prince
Herod his killer would lose his glory
his pompous kingdom sent spinning

to hell But talk of spinning
what an overturn in Jerusalem town
made a donkey's back a seat of glory
Did the lion of Judah conceal a lamb
in eyes that were hankering for a prince?
That blind man shouted out his descent

from David the king and in that descent
saw men and trees and birds spinning
out of his dark and the eyes of the prince
who opened his own Town
after town had seen the lamb
do wonders like that and want no glory

What foolish men are they who glory
in this dark Friday and their own descent
to the foot of the tree that holds their lamb
Do they see in his cross a spinning
stone? And dead men walking through the town
let out of prison by their prince?

From the godforsaken he sends spinning
his cry of sharing their dark descent
O lion and lamb in the heart of a prince

FOR STRONG GOSSAMER

My love for you now that I look at it
is wormriddled A widowed spider
who's eaten her mate alive

lairs at its centre And this hand
that might have held you or held you up
if it had been whole and wholesome

like I thought   now that I look at it
is blunted and dumb and leprous
What will I do with it? This poor thing

Will I take it to the keeper and say
O keeper this is meant to be my love
See how it putrefies And will

the keeper do as he's said to do   take
strong gossamer and net together
my love? web in the maggoty flesh?

Will he that keeper of love overlay
my kind with his kind? Can I pray
he will? I pray that I can

In the nighttime of the year
frost deepens and snow
muffles cricket whistles
cats curl their tails
and sleep and deep denned
bears dream of berries

From somewhere a call "News
"News" and a call back
"What news? What
"news for a dark season?"
It comes again "News
"Good news" and again
back "What news is good
"in the middle of the night?"

And in return across the eastern
sky the news always
good and always new
a star and morning

If you had a camel and you
could ride would you follow
those wise men back
east and east back
and back to where the star
first rose?

Would you hear
it sing with the sons of God
in the morning of the world?
itself a song of daysprings
yet to come?

If you listened well
would you hear great
great grandmother Eve
"Adam what did He mean
"when he said my seed
"would bruise the serpent's head?"
and Sarah laugh in her tent
"An offspring of ours will bless
"all families in the world?"
and Mary stop the angel voice
with wonder "How
"can these things be?"

If you had a camel and you
could ride   would you follow
that star and all wise men
to where it stays above
an innyard stable where donkeys
bray His praise and wonder
"Will the King ride
"on one of us?" If you
come all this way and see
and hear   you'd better
shout His praise or stones
will call it out from under
snow

"The news is good
"The news is new
"Morning has come Morning
"will come The King has come
"The King will come The King
"does come   His time
"is always always
"here and now"

Richard Outram

YOUNG MAN ENMESHED

I

She so deftly touched him, passing before him
With her milk-blue body, her nest of black hair
And her delicate merciless hands, that he dreamed
Of continually coupling with her there;

And awoke slowly, staring at four sad walls:
Until a candle's flame burned blue and he turned
To confront a lascivious presence, a lewd mask,
With the loveless gesture he had recently learned.

II

'Now I lay me down to sleep
Daemonic rendezvous to keep:
If there should come, before I wake,
Lust that no sleeping man may slake

To lie with me, I pray the Lord
Who was and is Incarnate Word,
Will succour me: will exorcise
My ravaged selves as I arise.'

INFANT

I
see
light. Like
smoke. Like blood
in water. Threading through,
about, from within
all things
Holy.

I
feel
sound. Like
shapes. Like motions
in water. Singing through,
about, from within
all things
Holy.

I
knew
Love. Like
music. Like fire
in water. Burning through,
about, from within
all things
Holy.

I
was
borne. Like
Life. Like Death
in Life. Seeping through,
about, from within
all things
Holy

I
am
Now. Like
Death. Like Life
in Death. Pulsing through,
about, from within
all things
Holy.

BITTERSWEET

The more we take, in every lengthened year,
Of your stained fruit, the more you branch and bear:
The thorn is dead, constricted by your vine,
That lifts your life to light, but not in vain;
You hang above our hearth-fire and we muse
Upon the cold flame of your broken blaze,
To suffer contradiction; which can both
Reprove us, for the falsehood of our truth
And like the wounds, Self-evident, of Christ,
Thus misdirect us into Paradise.

VOCATIONS

Assassins, certain to be caught
But certain of at least one shot,
Obliterate all other thought.

Torturers who come to budge
Faith like mountains, bear no grudge:
Never question, never judge.

Hunters hungry for the kill
And scenting blood and panic still
Discipline rapacious will.

Cuckolds, husbanding their pain,
Swear they will not care again,
Once the paramour is slain.

None of us, not you, not I,
Thus instructed in the lie,
Ever needs to learn to die.

Yet even as we learn to thrive
On death, the better to survive,
Truly, Love, we come alive:

To test the vast substantial thought
And Prayer of Spenser, being taught
' . . . the merveiles by thy mercie wrought.';

Or echo Milton's echo sent
To choir the blinding Dove's descent,
That we might see all passion spent;

Or watch a monstrous Shakespeare gauge
Upon an inward kindled stage,
Lear's irrevocable rage

And the Arcadian Marriage feast,
Where we are celebrants at least,
Transfiguring the twoback beast;

Or worship, ardent with Jack Donne,
Lest Maidenhoodwink Three in One,
To Sacramentalize the Pun;

Or with deft, gentle Herbert take
Up paradox and praise, to slake
A poet's thirst for sweet Christ's sake;

Or witness Blake with Angel Sword
And naked Babe in One accord
Emend himself with Holy Word;

And Human, radiant, embrace,
Assume and suffer, face to Face,
Our own Annihilation, Grace.

OTHER

Man being man, ingenious in disguise,
Familiar in the part, however much
He apes himself abandons otherwise;
Wills to be man and recognized as such.
Man being God is error's commonplace:
Authority usurped cannot evade
Resemblance; we see ourselves embrace
Misprisioned power in naked self-parade.
God being Man entrusted into time
Is Personal, our present focused whole
Body of history, the Human paradigm
And Sacrament, our passionate last role
Identified, to magnify and laud
Man become Man. God being God is God.

✚ 183

Jay Macpherson

THE INNOCENTS

Bloody, and stained, and with mothers' cries,
These silly babes were born;
And again bloody, again stained, again with cries,
Sharp from this life were torn.

A waste of milk, a waste of seed;
Though white the forest stands
Where Herod bleeds his rage away
And wrings his bloodless hands.

THE NATURAL MOTHER

All the soft moon bends over,
All circled in her arm,
All that her blue folds cover,
Sleeps shadowed, safe and warm.

Then lullaby King David's town,
The shepherds in the snow,
Rough instruments, uneasy crown,
And cock about to crow,

And lullaby the wakeful bird
That mourns upon the height,
The ancient heads with visions stirred,
The glimmering new light;

Long rest to purple and to pall,
The watchers on the towered wall,
The dreamland tree, the waterfall:
Lullaby my God and all.

THE FISHERMAN

The world was first a private park
Until the angel, after dark,
Scattered afar to wests and easts
The lovers and the friendly beasts.

And later still a home-made boat
Contained Creation set afloat,
No rift nor leak that might betray
The creatures to a hostile day.

But now beside the midnight lake
One single fisher sits awake
And casts and fights and hauls to land
A myriad forms upon the sand.

Old Adam on the naming-day
Blessed each and let it slip away:
The fisher of the fallen mind
Sees no occasion to be kind,

But on his catch proceeds to sup;
Then bends, and at one slurp sucks up
The lake and all that therein is
To slake that hungry gut of his,

Then whistling makes for home and bed
As the last morning breaks in red;
But God the Lord with patient grin
Lets down his hook and hoicks him in.

BUS STOP IN THE PRAIRIE DAWN

In the pearl half-light a mourning dove
murmurs like rain; in the road-dust, dew,
the sun-flowers raising their eastern look,
the ant-tunnel highway among the corn
fragrant with Eden —
               The day so new
nothing has fingered it, tossed the cup
crushed to the road-side.
               Day so pure,
even a breath is eucharist.

THE UNPROVED GLORY

How many believe? The text-books lie.
The simple Marthas shed
their knittings, name with vulgar tongue
the crazy angels as they come.
Even a child can see them.

The unproved glory itches us.
"No God," says one, "but an afterlife!"
"Only a good," says another, "None
but transient, changing, relative,"
another says, and one: "The state,
the folk, the general health!"

One, silent as in a station where all trains
wait without numbers, only waits,
sans journey-end, sans fare.
But in that waiting room a Truth,
limping, perhaps, like an old hound
that seeks a patch of sunlight, comes —
glory, perhaps. As the eye holds dust,
it itches us.

Well, viewed by the God
who's not lonely in the skies
and has, God knows, a sense of humour,
it's a humourous sight, each man in his,
each man in his own.

I've a stitch in my side
where they took Adam out;
I've not laughed so much since,
split a pang and I lost —
and Humour's gone, far wandering
where Dis, inspired,
runs hunting with his bell-voiced hounds;
than that one flower —
not in this world, a fairer.

I was wived by God
on the vanishing hill. Who broke
Pandora's greenhouse lid or wrote
that scissor scrabble on her stem,
on each leaf "time," "oblivion"?
And Humour ran out,
naked and fey.
"Look out, Sister Ann!"
cried Bluebeard's wife, locking
the opened door.

Well, viewed by the God
who's not lonely in the skies,
compost or dung — it's a humourous sight,
like the seed on the plate
in the closed-up yard.

But taste and eat —
and Adam dies.
Was it Eva's fault
that cost her then,
or Humour's bent
that separated Bluebeard's lock,
split leaf from stalk,
each man in his own,
that cost her all that sorrow
for that flower sought
dissociate, distinct,
and, God knows, lonely,
in all those worlds and skies?

THE BANDERLOG

How odd that from this natural, this
churning, puppy-bath of life,
God's monkey-thought spouts up, is us.
The white-throat sparrow song
appears more proper from its throat
than our bach bark from battle grass,
yet animals hang round our farms
concentric to our homeliness.
Baloo, Bagheera have their own;
why should the banderlog essay?
With what extraordinary grace
God's furless comics fall from grace,
strike harshly on themselves, and rise
sleek as the rats from the river murk
into His awkward, animal, and, thus,
forgiving day.

Theodore Colson

CHRIST THE FLESH

Christ the Flesh
And Christ the Word
And oh the worm in my leching and lying
Sweet flowers blow
And night breeze blossom
Christ! the ache in my arms.

"I believe"
But flesh flourishes its idolatry.
Sweet lady, when she flowers in the night
Christ, I have no care of you.

I could have no care of you,
Except that your body's Resurrection
Is in my words, Word.
If you are Love and Truth, and I say truth,
My unseemly words become you.
For no true word is not flesh
Of your body.
And that leching love I stammered
Which she, my goddess, thought only lying
My God, was you.

Christ the Flesh and Christ the Word
Bread and wine and windy weather
When I lay me down this night
Blossom
And still whisper.

LADY BUG

I have been reading about the entropy of the universe,
How it's all running down to death,
When a lady bug interrupts me.

Ladybird, ladybird, fly away home
Your house is on fire and your children are gone,
An old charm to be said
Since it's bad luck to kill a lady bug.

A friend to man, they eat aphids.
Some places farmers go into the mountains to collect them.

A curious name:
Our Lady's bird.

She settles on my finger,
Spreads her orange shells, which glow translucent in the lamplight,
And unfolds surprisingly long delicate wings,
Then whirls in a crazy looping flight,
And daintily pulls her wings back in again.

Emerson said to the rhodora
Beauty is its own excuse for being,
But Burrough's Naked Lunch serves up
An egg containing a nasty object, an orange containing only a huge
    worm
Once, on K.P., I went to clean behind a cupboard
And found about a thousand big cockroaches swarming.

Baalzebub, Baalzebub,
There are sights
That almost make us suspend our decision about
                        the propriety of devil worship,
And the expediency of conciliating the devil.

I have been reading of sharks.

But the funny lady bug
Interrupts
It has no message from Our Lady
And yet Our Lady interrupts
For contemplation of a small, odd perfection.

Lady bird, lady bird, fly from my hand
Tell me where my true love stands
Uphill or downhill or by the sea sand
Lady bird, lady bird, fly from my hand.

RESONANCE

A student told me,
Echoing professors,
"None of the proofs of God's existence are valid."
Another says
"There are no intrinsic values."

I am listening
To the frost's crystals
On the grass blades
In the moonlight.
Your cold hand
Holds me to the earth —
Almost I can hear its heart beating.

Wind, Wind, in the branches,
Wind, Wind in the hedgerow,
Wind in the tall grasses,
Who do you whisper
As the frost forms?
God is
I said
A principle of order.

"How do you know?"

Is there a voice in the whirlwind?
Is there a voice in the earthquake?
What does the fire say?
Or in the ice crystals creeping on the dark, still pool?
Now in the river's falls
Covered in cascades of ice
There is a murmur yet.

"There can't be any value
Unless somebody wants something."
"Man invented God
But now knows better."

I am listening for a small voice
I hear the sleet
Murmuring, rattling, whispering
Down hard on the surface of the snow.
Or, softer,
Crystals sifting down.

I hear wind in the spruces,
The dark sky scudding.

I hear the snow settling
Layer on layer
In the chasm
Of McCallum Brook.

At the top of an old spruce
Three ravens caw, and croak, and creak,
And one will fly up and hover
With a voice like a squeaking gate
And settle
And another flutters his great fingery wings.

John Ditsky

ON GOOD FRIDAY

On Good Friday, our Good
Friday, the sun shone
and the frogs sang antiphons;

the geese blew roadster
horns and the skunk cabbage
ruffled upward out of stream
beds. And if this was nearly
all — this and the woodpecker's

prospecting — there would be
more to come. For the Lord
went winking to his grave.

VOYEUR

He walks alone within his empty house
of dark and shadows (lamps outside? or suns?)
quite naked: it's a ritual of self.

Though no one sees him — for he'd think the sight
of him observed by other eyes absurd —
he sees himself self-seeing, and approves.

The play of light upon his skinny frame,
the hint of leaf on flesh, is nothing bad;
he knows his limits, knows his absences

of grace, yet loves enforced *is* of *as*:
thinks candor justifies his lonely stroll.
In short, he loves himself (for all his hate

of all he means to be) as no one loves
him, and as no one knows his love. He thinks
he understands the bland acceptance God

must feel for all created things, as is;
or else, in eye of mind, he sees the ease
of sending spirit out to walk along the shore.

SEPTEMBER EVENING BICYCLE RIDE

nights come early now   cooler
ending of a warm day   smooth
motion   balanced rolling line

reality fragmented by movement
panes of glass   tree branches
reordered by movement   spun
like cannisters   cylinders full
of lucky tickets   random art
metaphor of the spinning spokes

the mind set out to cool   like
a pie in a comic book   stolen
by bits of glimpsed and savored
life   colors   bodies   pictures
on the walls of strangers   odd
noises and musics   summer scent

good neighborhood in a bad town
precious bits assembled mosaic
stained glass   we worship here

SUCH LOVELY

In this family, nothing is wasted.

I wear a dead man's shirt —
It is my size, exactly. He
Was a leisured priest, maltreated
Rusticated unpromoted by an Irish
Bishopric. (Could pick no Daisy;
Gatsbyed instead in shirts.)

He left me nothing but his blessing,
I presume. And indirectly, this his
Shirt — a leisure shirt. In it,
And mirrored, see me waver between
A blessing (hieratic, sacerdotal)
And the thought of loss, missed chance.

Nothing is wasted in this family.

EL TESTIGO (for Patricio)

Senor, me has mirado los ojos;
Sonriendo, me has dicho mi nombre.
En la arena he dejado me barca.
Junto a ti, buscare otro mar.

> — *Chilean hymn, courtesy of*
> *my friend Howard Richards*

I

once a week
we ride together after school
through parking lots and alleys,
and, locking our machines,
ascend four flights of stairs
in a building that refuses
to announce itself

once a week
he has chosen to study the tongue
of his seafaring ancestor
whose bones have mulched two hundred years
beneath the sod of his mother's country,
a captain, marrier of migrant tongues,
progenitor of revolutionaries, yankees,
true believers

he does not care that his name translates
well, *Pedro Manuel,*
nor that the tongue of his ancestor
was spoken by Kaballists, martyrs,
inquisitors, *conquistadores,*
believers all,
in something
he only wants to visit his friend
who does not speak much English

so once a week
we ride, we climb,
process along the locker-lined hall
in this country of possessions and refuge
and open a door:

"Ola! Peter!"

II

when I who am his mother
return
light blazes from the single room
at the top of the building
onto a playing field long since filled with absence,
and spills along the locker-lined hall:

"Ciao! Peter!"

we descend, we exit
from one of many double mouthed doors,
release the combinations that chain
our shadow-thin machines,
and lightless, gearless,
glide *con cuidado*
the darkened labyrinth of sidewalks,
alleys, parking lots,
and remember those who have left their boat in the sand
and disappeared
in the country of the voice that announces
once a week:

"Ola! Peter!"
"Ciao! Peter!"

One thing leads to another:
you do this (good thing) then that.

Oh virtuous woman, whose sheets are white,
who dips her husband's robes in purple,
whose children's clothes are mended,
waiting for the visitor (who never comes)
when all things —
  the dinner hot
  the counters clean
  fresh beds plumped —
have been accomplished in the order
remembered, longed for
in the childhood she imagines
she can find, has lost,
this perfect vision.

When you return to the gallery
the picture is not the same
as you remembered it.

Yet you remain its victim,
triggered by things,
the thick smell of August;
the tinny high friction of crickets
rises and falls with the feel of the wind,
the shadows of a momentary cloud,
and you possess more than the memory
of what might have seemed a passing cup
(take it or leave it but you always took):
how surprising, appalling these moments have been
but now they just are.

The voice inside you
calls out so deeply now
it is unutterable to the things of your doing
and you are glad in the sadness
of this great divide
where once you raged with your fist on the wall
where now you come
on your knees.

DRINA JOUBERT 1914–1985

I

Yes
"Drina Joubert"
is written in my notes,
we were expecting you,
you and Gail from Sistering.

You ate little, but
called me to a table
you had found
of other Francophones
from Scotland, Africa
(and who knows where
in this assorted land)

and made me cry
when you told me the iris
I had bought at the very last minute
was your mother's favourite,
How Lovely
Real Flowers
you'd said

but would not take them home
because nothing was nice
in the place where you stayed.

II

Tonight a year later
I read in the paper
your mother has died
and your frail frame found frozen
in the wreck of a truck

not even donkey or dung
to give you heat
so you have gone home.

III

Limbs light as petals
on the waves of Mary's blue sleeves
flesh rosy from love, now borne
like Jesus
Drina Joubert
may yet save us
from the freezing
in our hearts.

Gail Fox

ABSOLUTES

If there is genius,
then it is everyone,
and not this pallid
suffering of the deities

bound to shoes and
shirts and second-hand
wings that cannot
elevate.

Lord, give me wings
that will get me up, and
if I crash, give me
the courage of spilled blood.

But do not make me
half-genius, half-idiot,
so that I cannot learn
Your absolutes.

WORKSHOP

In this workshop,
we learn to build

Birdhouses with
holes too large for birds

Too small for humans

Holes we cannot squeeze
through

That birds cannot plug
with straw

Holes that are energy
leaks, claptrap visions of the
world

The world being these
houses, ready to explode

God give us houses of
sanity

Or let us be, God,
wholly what we are

Personally, God, your
dreams that made us are
Frankenstein

Or was it us, God,
who made these bird-houses,
these holes

Of infinite awkwardness,
wobbling like cripples in the
broken air

Chips fly like dynamite
Someone is building a monstrosity

Let him build, Lord,
and help us all

With the houses of
our insanity

With the houses of
our love and terrible calm

The fourth wall opens
and sun comes through like
birdsong; what am I? I ask
trying to write of sorrow,
for in a flash

The light flew everywhere, and
I saw my history strangely
incomplete, changed by your
death, I saw solitude and endless
thinking, What am I?

Living or passing into death
like that, as you, running to a
prayer meeting, shouting,
dancing down the highway to
meet the Ultimate

In a flash of light, I saw
solitude or love, the next step
was walking through the forest,
and then the clearing, where
a group of people prayed and

Sang, as you did once, and
shook the cold spring off,
and I forgot the question I
had asked and joined in, as
round and round we danced

In the alphabet of prayer, and
leaped and danced until the
heart pounded and joy filled
the cold air with fire of the
holy spectrum and you were there

EASTER 1980

On being told by my younger child
that church is boring, you gasp and
visibly become the worst month
of the year, possibly January.

The honest statement hurts. Why did
you ask him with such passionate
attention? The sink water splashes,
the cheeks redden with exertion.

From day to day you live, straight
to the core of death and dying. You
stay up at night and never sleep. You
ask me life's meaning.

Don't ask questions you can answer
yourself. You with all your Christian
symbols. We're here to help each
other, I guess. My child smiles.

I share my loneliness. Lord, Lord
what days these are. Wishing that you
had a sense of humour. Or a bad memory, the
only kind to have. A changed vision.

THE BEGINNING OF CONTEMPLATION

(For Margaret Avison)

The countryside sparks and blazes, and
diehard leaves upon the branches burn with
the same intensity that collapses stars.

I tell you truly that now I know the shape
of goldenrod, that God, the fireball, against
a backdrop of deep pines, is sinking into my
head at the velocity of dark light.

From undisclosed sources, the pain in my
head is as quiet as overhanging grasses,
brown, frozen, stiff as driftwood from some
immense ocean.

This is the beginning of contemplation.
This, the sparkling rocks and golden
butterflies, is the living Jesus. Gorgeous
the sun over the slim legs of the evening.

THOMAS MERTON

1

As pink spread up the
pitted bark of elm in April,
I thought about men of genius
that I had known;

Those who addressed themselves
to Shakespeare's sonnets, and
those who lived a useless life
as Thomas Merton put it,

Who were bundles of beginnings,
who never read or wondered
what century it was or what
was the price of bread,

Who swore they would never
speak again, but hang in
silence from the thread of an
ear, and pray

The Muse would land them
safe with legs to walk on,
and a precise weather in their
heads to care.

2

In bony fire you sit,
a twig of wood aflame, burning
for the resurrection of the
Lord; in autumn how the leaves

Turn and swing on empty air!
The excited trees are whispering
of His approach, restless you
gaze out at the stars,

And are overwhelmed by sadness.
What is to be done? Your
exercise is in loving alone, and
O the perfume of the lilac —

Lord of the Dance, how the
rhythm of the stones lets the
purple blossoms through. But now
the flowers break off,

There is no place to meet you
anymore. I write this for you,
Thomas, to make a monk's joy
visible to the terrible world.

Anne Corkett

COLUMBA ON IONA

When he sailed from Ireland
Columba was steeled
to necessity, all administration's
fine activity, building, forging
converts, nailing them
into the structure, laying
his life as though he knew
it was a cornerstone. There were
no distractions and he was not then
a saint. But when he saw
a great crane
fall
and lie
still and white
as a stone on bare Iona
he knew instantly what it is
to be blown far off course
and he said

       Sleep
and in my sorrow take your rest
for into the exhausted places
comes the hope for nothing
on earth. One who has come
so far from home is blessed.

       And for three
days Columba nursed the crane,
kept it from wind, fed it bread,
stroking the long throat, swallowing
with his hands his own need, his hands
working like water, insistent
as rain. And for two nights
he prayed the dream of a dove
returning. On the third
evening the bird lifted
its wings and flew out

of Columba's sea-grey eyes west
toward Ireland. And Columba prayed
never to lose sight, never
to look back.

Nearly a century later, Adamnan,
writing his Life of St. Columba,
recorded miracles, foretellings
of future events, which perhaps owed
much to Adamnan's power of imagination.

TEMPORAL ZONE

What ever forever is
I'm not sure I want
to go there even
separated from pain
and transformed, given
what good there is
to work with made all;

I'm not sure unless
the good can puddle off
to join a common pool,
redistribute itself,
evaporate to atmosphere;

that would be useful
being distilled into
a sort of beneficent dew

though it would mean
coming back down again

but I suspect forever
precludes re-entry

seeing as the twinges
of foreverness that come
pull out toward sundown
or what's back behind sun-up.
Considering I know how and when
the sun rolls round
     that it does
sets up a long ache unsettlingly
often
  which says
cold hard information's no
help and though getting
it's diverting
    being
distracted from eternity
is useless and not something
I'd want for friends
or favourite landscapes.
     This evening
taking place outside the window
has a splendid uselessness
barring the notion
of all things gathering
toward rest touched
by splendour.

IN CAPERNAUM

I sat down on the edge
of a hill thinking
                    I
          have
climbed, am still
aware of heights
                    can
          take
stock and exercise
critical judgement
                    which
          says
I have climbed this
far and if
                    I
          go
farther
may
                    become
          rareified
fined out
with light,
                    breathing
          scarce
and thin, dizzy
with objectless
                    aerial
          accomplishment
and disappear
from the weighty
                    world
          go
it along. Christ
in the wilderness
                    knew
          that
one and
the other
                    just
          sitting
watching

the show
                    not
          even
taking it in
just sitting watching
                    the
          hoop-
la fan-
dango devil
                    show
          but
hearing
that John
                    was
          arrested
He turned back
settled in Capernaum
                    and
          then
there was no choice
                    and
          then
there was no rest
for God and all
                    His
          angels
gave
Him voice.

John Reibetanz

APPLE

This last bite
opened a door
into the core,
peeling night

from a sleeping pair
of seeds. How calm:
pure son, pure daughter
fresh from God's dream.

When rank grass hissed
and their own whispers
tunnelled air
with the first nightmare,

Did Adam and Eve
fall to the fruit
as in retreat
to the womb of love?

THE CONTRACTOR

When God made me, there was a war on:
Supplies were scarce, so He did it on the cheap.
Oh, not that He produced a moron
Or paraplegic by starving my fetal sleep —

No, He laid a solid foundation
Of bone and tissue for the little house. (If Mother
Smoked like a chimney through my gestation,
That's free will, not His fault, and I'm sure He'd rather

She hadn't). It was not on the basic structure
But on pricier options He stinted. After the unlicensed
Plumbing burst in an early rupture,
The narrow air ducts blocked with asthma, and I sensed

At the second or third attack that I'd be
Spending my whole life paying for His penny-wise
Pound-foolish sense of economy.
And what kind of contractor, if any, buys

Windows so worthless a horn-rimmed casing's
Required to make them work? Or a double door
That won't shut without metal bracings?
I would have taken a loss and moved out, but for

Something I found in the attic: a box
Crammed with words of all description — brick ones,
Finely-scrolled wooden ones, intox-
Icating, flowing silky ones. The fictions

I framed with those words were more than enough
To make the place liveable, though it's taken time:
New front, new walkways, costly stuff
Growing around the foundations. Now that I'm

Renovated, I plan to expand
The business: all (townhouses, exotic
Holiday villas, commercial and
Industrial parks) nothing if not chic.

In fact — why keep my great end dim? —
My ultimate goal, in ten-point boldface print's
A God more opulent than the chintz-
Y one who framed me. Or the one who penned Him.

GREAT HOUSE, SOUTH AFRICA

Surely among a rich man's flowered lawns
At half-past ten you'll find the gardener sweating
From hauling turf since five. The master yawns
Over his balconied breakfast, still regretting
Last evening's lost *bon mots*. While distant fawns
Flash in the sunlight of a timeless setting
Kept by dark, nameless hands, perhaps it dawns
On him, sipping the ebony cup and staring
At a box-hedge chess set never meant for sharing,
That, but for constant, unacknowledged shearing,
The king would sit no higher than his pawns.

Before I start, would some of you young fellows
Throw open the windows? It wouldn't do
To hibernate when all the rest of the world
Opens its eyes at the tender urging
Of spring sunshine: even our slow old ash —
My brother! — is sporting little green buds this morning.

Now you can smell the sweetness of new life
Burst from the earth; and did you see
Those daisies set a gold crown on the hill
Across the road? So many gifts!
But I'm going to talk about one we overlook,
Not great like trees or glorious like flowers: grass.

Grass is always with us, it never fails us:
Grass feeds the beasts, and they feed us;
It clothes the meadows, and in the early morning chill
Its breath mingles with ours as we work.
Its green colour rests the eye, and after
A long day the feel of it rests the body.

Perhaps it's time to root this grass in a text.
Here's my text: just "the grass of the field."
In the Book of Kings these words tell us how little
Man's power amounts to; but Christ lets them show
How much God gives us, dibbling the grass with flowers
That pass, but sowing man with the seed of love.

And our Lord's "much" sorts well with Kings' "little";
We and the grass are of small power,
Both green in the morning, as the Psalm says, and wrinkled
By evening — I'm proof of that — yet God
Has covered the earth with us, out of his skies fall
Showers of rain for the grass and mercy for man.

How little the grass is, measured against our much!
Moving but never leaving its place,
Grass wears the beauty of youth but never feels
Its passion; that's why nature-worship
Never answers our needs: how could we give
Our hearts to a god not free to love and suffer?

I think Christ must have found the grass a comfort,
Lightening his work and his sufferings,
And maybe he cocked an ear to catch the music
That spent stalks make with the wind
When they wither standing; or watched an autumn's red
Sunset reflected on millions of shining dry bents.

That's a sight you still may look for at harvest-time,
When the earth has rendered up its tithes
And the sun's rays come level with the ground; I saw it
Every night of the week when my boy
Was carried home from the war to die — a man's
Senses be sharp when his blessings be slipping away.

But it's spring, and the Bible calls spring grass "tender," not sharp —
Tender to the jaws of the young calves
In their first pasture, tender to an old man's mind.
It grows out of our deepest sorrows
And spreads fresh green, even over mounds
Of black earth turned by the spade in a stone's shadow.

It's time we picked up that "much" and "little" again.
Christ, who made much of the little of Kings,
Comes to us now, and makes our much seem little:
New-risen grass brings much comfort,
But Christ new-risen brings life the August sun
Can't wrinkle, and the fall's frost will never chill —

Eternal life, God's dearest gift to man,
Bought with the blood of his only son;
A crown that Kings would trade their riches for,
But one that's ours just for the asking:
So let the tender grass open your senses
To spring, and let spring open your hearts to Christ.

Margo Swiss

WHEELS

Wheel within a wheel is
we'll within a Will is
why we in hours
are yours.

In time, in place begun
wheel and we'll become
both together won.

So we'll, together one,
another wheel become
and willing, we'll wheel
to You.

TWOEDGED

Hebrews 4:12

I

I am dying to be
cut through of

hate, Love
lust, Love

paring us both down
to fell me cleanly.

You will no part hurt but
prune only

make then soul trim
this rude strung son.

II

Persist, Love;
draw me.

Beat
thinner than ever

my rock heart climb
smite (as You can)

sword-
like.

III

The Word
reflexive

brandishing Himself
is

raised
in two hands

joints ringing under
marrow sprung from

slavery though
slain even.

I THIRST

Liquor, my Lord, is Yours
poured on me from You
when very dry
dry as stones are dry by rivers
with spaces between the stones
(which we are also like)
being sometimes separate yet
both thirsting.

As I look up
your cup looks me back again
reflects from Whom I drink
myself by dryness drained.

Wine drenched from a vessel
revives
which when uplifted draws
best when empty
most full when dry
thus drunk, my Lord, am I.

IN PAIN OF SCHISM: MARY SPEAKS

I

First it was a kind of pruning
as from a tree
the child cut from me
dilated, dumb, eyes large
hands upon him
performed later
confinement, most final
entombment from which
neither life, nor breath, nor any created thing might pass
since dead he was
disposed of thus
in rocky ground.

II

Lightning before thunder
revealed the wonder
the load of his love interred
at dark
in spite of night
the stone shone
burned as on the head
cool and slow (they said)
burned as fire upon the hair
without air since
it was known
there was none there.

But where
(mother in me)
do they go after
milk drops
flesh knots
not needed, empties
grows slack after
birth: bits of blood only
wreck of the womb?
Put him in the tomb over there . . .

III

Remember, O God, the gums
gone down like a trap
drew me up and back
that reckless head
wanting a bed
felt like a vessel full of his clay
painstaking way he began
in rings
he moved outside and across
he came to a head
hard as a nail slammed into wood
was dead
too fast to prepare
the tear rent everything
I was.

Susan McCaslin

THE BEAUTY OF THE LAW

1

God is no dull monarch
Dispensing arbitrary forgiveness
But Law himself, written into
The very structure of atoms,
The way we breathe,
The tables of our hearts.

Law is the invariable
Order of the world.

2

A righteous man comes
Among us to suffer
and to die

The magic unwinds
The code decodes, the
Spell unspells his name.

God has placed within us
A plumbline:
One straight line.

Lamblike, matter
Explodes the tomb
Leaving the graveclothes
Undisturbed.

3

If the righteous man
By will walks through
The door of death:
He lives.

For Law is Justice
To those the Law
By Love makes just.

JOHN OF THE CROSS II (Cautery)

The cautery that wounds to heal
is with you in your hands.
The invisible ray

that penetrates my dark
is making a path in my heart,
as in your heaven.

In you is no dark —
is necessity of love.
The wound you make to heal

is no privation, no wound.
Only in the blithe inspirited
wind is my heart dancing.

Not from the deep,
not from the parting curtain
of sea and land; heaven and earth,

but from behind, within,
your eyes blaze beatitudes.
You are sovereign ever

of my innermost parts,
sanctifying flesh,
making it clean.

"And from thence he arose . . . and entered into a house, and would have no man know it: but he could not be hid." (Mark 7:24)

Though he walked precariously in the garden,
His body brushing mauve and white blossoms,
The hyacinths, the nodding lilies;
Though he passed early each day the lanes
Where merchants basked their wares in the sun,
Weaving invisibly among the village children
And on to the far, brown, rounded hills —
The man of God could not be hid.

His shining fringed the atmosphere with gold,
And the widows, the children, the labourers
Came begging, borrowing, pilfering
The hope that marched through Judea.

Slowly the pain for these lost
Gathered in his eyes, broke,
And with his death he released them
To his, their Father.

His crucified form floats now in their dreams,
Sighs in the countenances of the oppressed
Still struggling for impracticable ideals.
The dreamers, the poets and the musicians,
All those who could play the music
Have not forgotten him.

Though the machine hates the man of God
And crucifies him still on the bland millstone of time,
There is within each striver
A resurrected man of light,
Buried, but not hid,
A face to meet the faces,
Fearless, impregnable, enduring.

THE PATTERN OF THE CITY

There is a great dream
of a place not a place —
ou topos — no where — utopia.

The Muse of Plato knew
disintegrated man
could not govern himself;

yet to be governed
by imperfect men
ends only in tyranny.

Sun-dazzled philosopher
returns to time's cave,
sees men as monsters chained.

You must remake yourselves,
move to the tabernacle
pitched by the King.

Always the just man
is the cornerstone
of the just city.

The shining pattern
in the soul of one
revives utopia for all.

Does it matter that
the ordered city
lives only in the mind?

Not if the mind
is a place of creation
a necessary world.

O city planners you must
burn your blueprints
for technical progress,

give up your magic,
watch your Babel fall
into many-tongued confusion

before you can hear the music
of the city that rises
from its dust.

Glenn Hayes

FOR THE TEACHER WHO RECONCILES ALL
BEING WITH TIME

You did not say that history was fake;
that toothache was a sign of some
huge cosmic serpent chewing on its tail;
that death was a sentence for trafficking
in fingers and eyes.

          True, time,
like a great ferris-wheel, tumbles seasons,
days, and all divergent being
in woeful cycles; yet a circle,
in this world of wounded sense, will serve
most easily as symbol for
eternity; and symbols, so
you taught, were necessary signs
of life; which to prove, you called
yourself the Word.

          You taught that history,
though it wove a dizzy spiral, spun
finally to an end; that suffering,
even slight, could be offered to redeem;
that death, in you, was finishing work
for fingers, eyes that from the very start
were meant for glory-rides.

IN REVERSE

Alone on this road to Salonika   where ricocheted
sun shimmies asphalt into air
and sky seems the easiest opening to home

I wander waist-deep into golden lakes
of wheat   to glean from broken chaff
a parable to right the toppled world

I cannot imagine comfortable foxes
sedentary doves   nor the homeless-happy
Son of Man   but recall only the

last time in Salonika   when I sold to an old
man for his dying son   a pint of my blood
Above the field   the road dissolves

in the sky the sun stops   then reverses
I feel the very print of Christ
smudged in my heart

DENIALS

The desert   like a breathing corpse
exhaled a frigid sigh that crept
across the cactus land of rock
through gateways of the night-charred town
through labyrinths of narrow streets
to settle in a walled courtyard

There   withered branches waiting for
the fire rattled like dry bones
and men pulled cloaks tight round their necks
Blossoms in the garden trembled
fragrance froze   each bloom withdrew
and tightened to a bud of pain

Workers and police milled restless
scowled at unreasonable cold
and built a fire of dry sticks
('Where I go you cannot follow'
he said   But the rock was solid)

'Wait a little   a little while
it will warm in a little while'
someone said   A sound   violent
and sharp   echoed through the courtyard
The mob fell silent   listening
but they heard nothing   just voices
rattling officious in the dark

The fire threw shadows on the wall
scattered light on random faces
'You there' said a maid   (he stepped back)
'You were with him in the garden'
'Untrue' he did not hesitate
to say   And again and again
he said it in the uproar that
ensued   for   brothers   what is truth
after all?   Deep blue greyed to dawn
and he withdrew to cold shadows
by the wall   The cock crew   He cursed
burst into tears   The fire guttered

Tim Lilburn

CALL TO WORSHIP IN A MASS FOR THE LIFE
OF THE WORLD

Come you with desire and you without desire
    and you high with the aplomb of the cared-for mad.
Come you who violently wait.
Come you brow bejewelled with the cranial ache to eat
                — bright, mental food — the world.
You sowing in tears, come.
Come you sleepless ones who hear in the clank-tappa-clang of un-
stable titanium heads
    banging walls of siloes in wind-boistrous Dakota
        spirit-rappings of your own garrulous deaths, come; come
           now.
Come all who are infatuated.
Come you who are Hamlet-spooked.
Let the jails empty
And let come diddlers, two-years-less-a-day sniffers
            with drooling sleeves.
Come fathers whose shame hands have burnt on breasts of Oh-eyed
    daughters
        in houses mortgaged at twenty per cent.
Come. Let the electric locks release.

Come you dangerous ones who have seen all that is solid melt into
    air.
Into the hearing of these extravagant promises.
Come from the doughnut stands, the Trail's End Taverns.
Come you Vespuccis of the Americas of the eye.
Come, come now here to the peacelands and their white peninsulae
              which are hands raised, pax.
You seldom Nathaniels with leaping tongues, come.
The night eats towards us, its boot full of blood.
Dead Alden, poet, come, come from the night, the dead cough of your
    laugh gruffing
        as the large-animal-feeding sound of sea gnawing rock, your face
        of smoke,
            your head blurred with Player's Fine Cut's broken gold rings,
            come.
Brother William, painter, ex-crazy Ukrainian, come;

your bum callused by a father's deranged hand,
     settle it in pant-polished oak.
Come women with scars.
Come mumblers after quarters, with your newspaper shoe shuffles
     from the high-heeled, well-healed, Dior-cheekboned streets.
Come from the Thrift Villa, Mister Donuts, sanatoria, buckets.
Come child from the video parlour, your hands agog
      with the miracle of deke and thrust that outwhizzed the
        machine.
Come you who believe the golden M of the blood meat bar
   is all that remains of metaphysics, gold standing ruin of M, and
   that what
     lies behind the gold ruin is nothing,
       night-nothing, alive simply in its anarchically pure impulse
         of its hate of you,
    just night, glued one by the gore of insects exploded
         on the flashing windshields of the traffic.
Come, turn and come; bolt from the loveless cars idling in the street,
    doggying wearying tails of smoke.
Come you with child and you without child
And you whose children are your own nursed selves.
Come into the held breath of the mute God, who,
        seeing you, covers his face in awe.

CELEBRANT'S GREETING

Children, we are aristocrats
Fathered in the intimate wilderness of the Divine Name.
We have loved death. We have. We have pried warm tongues
Into the milky knot of death's blue lip,
Lacing the bored, otherwise yawning bone face.
We have loved Death and the face of Death
And Death has laid down with us.
Each of us, still, has been given a secret, white stone
From the baked, salt floor of God's absence.
And on this is written our living name.
Let us stand now here, and hold the name,
                    and eat the half-human wheat, the beating wine.

We have asked for a prophet and been sent our hunger.
O taste and see.

The barn floats
over its stone foundations
with a butterfly's inner expanse of self-estrangement,
over your milk flowers, weightless with arousal.
In its green, tilting ear,
the meadows of your flesh May-out.

Hegel knew this: Duns Scotus:
One or two of the prophets: when a beater on the New Idea manure
    spreader
hits a field stone money-center, the parabola the stone inquires
    through air
is the mind of the stone, and the mind-hiccup thinks, "I am in love
with the earth and the glory of men."
Listen.   Swan nose-heads in an Isadora Duncan neck curl.
Theo-erotic, see the wills of discrete objects touching as hands.

Now in the meeting house rustle and cough of the eating barn
                the most Bach-organ-like shadows
are the elongated blues cast by your udders at the pale risings of milk
    — G
chords of the absence of light.
In the cloud, God dwells.
Oh blank out Death, yurodivetsvo, I tell you, the absence with the
    lips of Victor Mature
washing-machining up and down. I have hauled some of you stiff
from the mustard-coloured floor. I know.
What is the urge to implode self,
bones and blue mouths of muscle
into the white lake in you
but a desire for heaven?
The barn sways and lives and has being in the living ghost of your
    pump tubes.   O.

Barry Dempster

DROWNING

There are people weeping into
Bibles, smudging the print, crying
because Jesus fades. They're sitting
on the edge of the world as
if it were a bed, shoes half-off,
dangling into space. There is
no faith left, no barefoot place in
their hearts. Rooms are grey, like nests,
pages thick with twigs and mud. They
sit, half-blind Bibles sopping wet,
little children welling over
in their eyes. The children are
perfect copies of themselves
before their crying.

He talks to some of them, wades in
their tears, says things about light, dry
spells, how together they could soak
up oceans. Their eyes flicker, the
kids fidgeting, so quick to
believe. Their Bibles fall, go
under. They open their mouths to
speak. Words held back by angels.
Angels as dry as sun.

I lie on my back, drifting, most
of my body submerged. There are
no islands. I watch the clouds, the
shapes they take, what life was once,
before all the water. People
tell me the tops of trees
separate us from sky. They say
it's in the Bible. But when I
look, all the words have been wept
away. On the shiny blank pages
I see my own reflection.

BELIEVING IN BILLY

Hong Kong, Sydney, New York, amongst
thousands of uplifted faces
a man stands on stage
beneath dreamy lights.

Microphone in his mouth.
Bellowed psalms. Proverbs of
universal tongues.

His hands hold tight to
a gleaming Bible, the
world smoothed, compressed like coal.

Are those angels in his eyes
blue with hope, squeezed small as stones?

His is world-loved, held
precious in a TV
camera's boxy arms.

The *Ladies Home Journal*
testifies him holier
than Christ. My mother, light-swept
in her soggy chair, swears he
is equal to John the Baptist.

Billy, when you swallow
at the end of prayer, are
you talking to God?

Will you raise your arms out-
stretched for just a moment?

Can you touch me, hand to
shoulder, a swooning dance?

Might you save a man
from choking on himself?

Your head is bowing through my
TV set, your hair streaked white
a halo tilted with the years.

I like to watch your hands
steadying the crowds, a
man with perfect posture.

And your eyes, I love to see
them drop into the Bible,
angels falling to their knees.

But TV always ends, living
rooms dry as plaster, the world
dark and fabric once again.

Where do you go, Billy?
You are a lot like God —
a flickering glimpse.

The TV set grows cold and
safe, the site of an ancient
miracle. A long-last heaven
of makeup and dreamy lights.

This night, a tongue-tied
prayer. Something to sustain
me, a microphone.

That same old prayer — can you see me,
see me . . . is anybody there?

1/

When Jesus broke the temple
mirrors, Judas lost his eyes
amidst the rubble. Peter began
to forget himself, while Mary
dug her fingers in the ground.

The sun winked once, a fallen
shard of glass reflecting
hurried feet, empty sky.

When Jesus crushed flowers in
the muddy garden, disciples
breathed rainbows in the sleepy
steamy air. Mary, far
away, combed and braided hair.

In the distant ruins of
a temple, people plotted,
fingers petrified. Eyes turning
black, bits of tarnished silver.

When Jesus slumped upon
the cross, Joseph built a
chair without a back. Judas
snapped a branch with the weight
of his falling body.

All the watchful faces,
darkly smooth, made wooden
grimaces instead of tears.

Mary saw a shooting star
burn grey, then disappear.

2/

Behind the clouds sun searches
for a holy man, an eye
rummaging for an empty socket.

Can we not forget
Christ died bit by bit?

Blind men believe they are
skin and bone. Infidels
lose their fingers in diagrams.

Scientists give Latin
names to long-dead stars.

Having faith in anything
until it disappears.

The world depending on
itself — blind men describing
mirrors . . . men and women sitting
back to back on broken chairs.

3/

God says faith is something grand,
unseen. Christ the invisible.

Standing in the centre of
a temple, silence multiplies
like glass. I walk in a
midnight garden, choking on
the smell of flowers. I dream
of a wooden cross, wake up.

It seems Jesus is
an empty place in my mind.

Faith more substantial than myself.

Maggie Helwig

A SECOND PROCESSION

See, we are blind as cavern fish
aimless as sharks
and even to know that we do not know
is past our knowing
and past all odds.

But this is true —
riding the ribs of our portable ark
in blood or water, we must stand and raise
our hands in a wild
absurdity of praise
children of this ill-mannered, audacious
foolish God.

The worship, the witness
of the fact — we offer
that we are. Hand, eye and bone
the voices that echo down the spiral stairways of our cells
the praise of the eyelid, the curious thumb
the stubborn muscle thumping the lungs, fibre and cartilage
dance of the skin in space, each lop-sided
face, wrong-measured limb.

The worship of earth, thick wealth of our prosperous mud
the worship of fire that strikes from our hands like flint
the worship of water, the devouring chill of the green
the worship of air, invisible demon of our desire.
The fruit and the mold, mushroom and weed, chrysanthemum
the metals that spark in the dark of the mines
the mind's-eye diamond, black pits of oil and coal
the rose in the forest.

We offer our colours, the soul-eating yellow of Arles, the sun,
the sunflower, cornfield, crows; and the yellow
of Turner's light, strapped to the beam of a sea-storm.
The music that shattered the heart of a saint in Milan, or ran
in the blood of the Saviour, El Salvador;
let our ears and eyes reclaim for Your images
these foolish images of the Face
we do not recognize.

Words that slide, slip and will not stay in place
the burnt taste in the mouth of each
adoring betrayal; daily we kiss You in the garden
dripping with myrrh.
Lord, bless our failures, wipe away our tears
welcome us home, accept and pardon
our worship, Lord.

THE CONVERSION OF ST. PAUL

"And Saul arose from the earth; and when his eyes were opened, he saw no man: but they led him by the hand, and brought him into Damascus. And he was three days without sight, and neither did eat nor drink."

The last boats shatter
on the flanks of God. And will
he speak soft words, or make a covenant with me
in the house of Judas
the belly of the sea?

There was a man
caught up to Paradise, who heard
words that he could not speak, saw things
he could not see for glory of the light —
I knew him once, this man.
He died.

In the house of Judas, with the masks of the dead (his eyes
are like the eyelids of the morning)
this third day, old men
have come to lay their hands upon my head.

(O lay not innocent blood on us, the sailors cried
as I fell on Damascus road.
And they cast me into the light)

Understand this —
in the last disaster of collapsing goodness
is no place for sight.
Ananias, can I say
on this third day you cannot change these eyes;
that if I rise
it is because we are both blind —
the colours of our irises, that
our weigh the sun?

Can I say
the one impossible thing is all
that has ever begun, that
before him we are destroyed, before him
sorrow is joy?

In the house of Judas, Ananias,
what can we say?

(And the men in the house of Judas said —
behold, he prays)

THE SECRETS OF ENOCH

And Enoch walked with God
and he was not.
And where he stood there was a shadow on the wall.
Angels take cords
and go to measure Paradise.

Long-fingered rabbis wrote that he had gone
to plead for fallen angels
and dead men.
Enoch stood in the mountain wreckage of the desert
and all the burnt day by the walls of Uruk
there was no sound.

The Watchers stare down in anxious fear
through crystal like a throne.
And he was not.

Angels take stones
and go to build Jerusalem.
In the night the shadow stands along the wall and says —
tell me of God.

David Creelman

TWO SONGS FROM TEN LEPERS

I

As he was going into a village
ten men met him
and called out in a loud voice

Wing shook
you scattered us
white like gulls
to the outer city piles
where we flap
in the dust
in the waste
with your blessing
in our bones.

II

One of them
seeing he was healed
came quietly back praising

Inside of me
you spoke your name
your breath
found my voice —
in my unraveling
you touch
into flight.

Mary's greeting
the baby leaped in her

Mother, in your womb
hard ripe and round
can you feel my kicking —
do you now feel me dreaming
of words in my mouth
thick as scrolls, soft as honey?
They will come from my lips
spreading fast as locusts
blacking the sun with wingbeats,
and they will stand as herders
driving the poor breaking
to the river.
I am folded in you
knees curled close
waiting to be straightened
dreaming of the washing
and the washed.

NOW WE ARE WAITING

After the third day we watch
the sun set red,
still mystic in ritual
awaiting the return
the reappearance of horizon;
breakings of land and sky.

Like believers between air and stone
we bend from beds, from places not beds,
to walk a clean dark.

Wanda Campbell

PRAYER

My man is going to be a fisherman
where sky is stitched with needling gulls
and beach is strewn with ribboned dulse.
His rhythm will be wave rhythm,
his wealth the wet and tumbling silver.
His dreams will be anemones
in vases of deep green glass,
his tears — brine.
He knows it is not enough.

Let him find you there in the cove
frying fish for him at dawn.
Meet him on the barnacled wharf
where once he wept.
Part the salt-tongued fog.
Hold out your sinewed arms
and still his storm.

CLAUDE

In winter I cut logs; in summer I
open a museum in my basement.

Tourists come up the Saguenay by boat
and see the sign painted big on the roof:

NATURE MUSEUM. A man from here does
taxidermy, but he calls it stuffing.

Three years we looked for birds and animals.
We fixed them up and arranged them nice with

branches and moss. Then François and Jean-Luc
gave us the shark they caught under the ice

one winter. Now tourists pay two dollars
to see. If they don't leave quick like they came

I take them to the church, everything made
from logs and roots — altar, benches, even

the Christ. Each man in the village
made something after the fire. Or I take them

up the mountain where you see everything,
the village, the woods, the river as far

as the Saint Laurent sometimes if it's clear.
After the long whistle the boat goes home.

Them that stay I take to the church and to
the mountain free of charge.

CHRISTMAS

On Christmas Eve we walked through Odell Park.
The architectural stillness, grey on white,
was broken by our voices in the dark.
Remembering, we spoke about that night
He climbed down a ladder of stars to Earth.
As we talked we made angels in the snow.
I recall what you said about his birth:
"Like the angels he's free to come and go."

The day after Christmas a warm wind came
bringing mist to the park and melting rain.
I returned to find nothing there the same —
only some swaddling rags of snow remain.
I searched the grass but could not find a thing;
those two angels had somehow taken wing.

NOTES ON CONTRIBUTORS AND POEMS

Avison, Margaret (b. 1918). Though born in Galt (now Cambridge), Ontario, she was raised in Western Canada and came with her family to Toronto as a teenager. After completing her B.A. (1940), she held various jobs and did freelance work. Her first collection, *Winter Sun* (1960), received the Governor-General's Award for poetry; it has been followed by *The Dumbfounding* (1966) and *sunblue* (1978).

¶ EASTER
  · *diapason* (1.5): melody, especially a burst of harmony.
¶ BRANCHES
  · *O Light* (1.5): cf. Acts 9:3–9.
¶ WATER AND WORSHIP: AN OPEN AIR SERVICE ON THE GATINEAU RIVER
  · *Joyful, joyful, we adore thee . . . .* (1.31): the title of a hymn, "words by Henry Van Dyke (1852–1933), sung to an Edward Hodges arrangement of Beethoven's 'Hymn to Joy.' " [M.A.]
¶ WE THE POOR WHO ARE ALWAYS WITH US
  · *shards* (1.7): pieces of earthenware.
¶ ALL YOU NEED IS A SCREW-DRIVER!
  · *title*: from television ad for *Idomo* furniture.
  · *anodynes* (1.1): medicine to relieve pain.

Bailey, Alfred Goldsworthy (b. 1905) was born in the city of Québec. After studies at U.N.B. (B.A. 1927) and Toronto (M.A. 1929; Ph.D. 1934), he held teaching positions (Professor of History and Anthropology) and administrative responsibilities at U.N.B. from 1939 to 1970. He has published a number of books, both scholarly and creative. His collected poems appeared in 1982 (Fiddlehead).

¶ TRUMP
  · *nones* (1.4): daily liturgical office originally said at the ninth hour (or 3 p.m.).

Beum, Robert (b. 1929) was born in Ohio, U.S.A., and immigrated to Canada in 1968. He has taught at several American and Canadian universities and now lives in Saskatoon. He has published widely as both a literary scholar and poet. His most recent collection of verse is titled *Celebrations* (1987).

¶ THE SOURCES
  · *sidereal* (1.15): of the constellations or fixed stars.
  · *staves* (1.21): stanzas.

Brewster, Elizabeth (b. 1922) was born in Chipman, N.B. She trained as a librarian and also in English literature (Ph.D., Indiana). Since 1972 she has been with the Department of English, University of Saskatchewan. She has published many books of poetry as well as novels and short stories.

¶ GOOD FRIDAY PERFORMANCE
Scriptural references in the poem include the following:
- *All we like sheep* . . . . (l. 43): Isaiah 53:6.
- *The sparrow hath found* . . . . (l. 48): cf. Psalm 84:3.
- *Lift up your heads* . . . . (l. 52): Psalm 24:7, 9.
- *The Lord will arise* . . . . (l. 64): Isaiah 60:2.
- *Behold, I show you* . . . . (l. 65): 1 Cor. 15:51.

Cameron, J.M. (b. 1910) was born in Manchester, England. He has taught at several universities in England (he was Chair of Philosophy, Leeds U., in 1960), and was University Professor, St. Michael's College, U. of Toronto (1971–78). He is the author of numerous scholarly publications, and his poetry has appeared in *Poetry* (Chicago), *TLS*, and *The Listener*. A collection, *The Music is in the Sadness*, is forthcoming from Porcupine Press.

¶ THE LYDIAN STONE
- *pinchbeck* (l.13): alloy of copper and zinc used in cheap jewellery.

¶ OF THE COMFORT OF THE RESURRECTION
- *Pythagoras, Plato* (l. 15): Greek philosophers whose philosophical systems elevated the soul above the body.

¶ THE RIDDLE OF THE STONE
- *Author's note:* This poem "is about the Eucharistic Sacrifice and presupposes the old form of High Mass with the principal celebrant ('the killer'), the deacon who reads the Gospel ('to publish the death'), and the sub-deacon who holds the paten ('the dish')."

¶ A CHRISTMAS THOUGHT FOR PIERRE RONSARD
- *Ronsard:* (1524?–1585) French poet.
- *rime* (l.1): hoar-frost.
- *farouche* (l.2): sullen, shy.
- *coneys* (l.4): rabbits.
- *Cueillir dès aujourdhuy les roses de la vie* (l. 15): from Sonnet XLIII, second book of the *Sonnets pour Hélène*.

Campbell, Wanda (b. 1963) was born in India, where she was also raised — the daughter of missionaries. She recently completed her M.A. at the University of Windsor and lives in Georgetown, Ont.

¶ PRAYER
- *dulse* (l.3): a kind of seaweed.

¶ CLAUDE
- *Saguenay, St. Laurent* (l.3, l.19): major Quebec rivers.

Cogswell, Fred (b. 1917) was born in East Centreville, N.B. He taught for many years in the Department of English and is now Professor Emeritus at the University of New Brunswick. His most recent publication is *Meditations: 50 Sestinas* (1986).

❡ THE CROSS-GRAINED TREE.
· *adze* (l.1): wood-cutting tool.

Colson, Theodore (b. 1935) was born in upstate New York and received his Ph.D. from the University of Michigan. He has taught at the University of New Brunswick since 1967 and has published one book of poems, *The Beauty of It.*

❡ LADY BUG
· *entropy* (l. 1): turning (in physics, a theoretical measure of energy).
· *Emerson* (l. 17): Ralph Waldo Emerson (1803–1882), American philosopher and writer.
· *rhodora*: a kind of shrub.
· *Burroughs* (l. 19): William S. Burroughs (b. 1914), American writer and author of *Naked Lunch*.
· *Baalzebub* (l. 23): usually Beelzebub; Satan or any devil.

Corkett, Anne (b. 1944) lives near Claremont, Ontario. She is the author of *Between Seasons* (Borealis, 1981) and *The Salamander's Laughter* (Natural Heritage, 1985), a children's book.

❡ COLUMBA ON IONA
· *Columba*: Irish missionary (521–597 A.D.) who converted Scotland to Christianity.
· *Iona*: small island of the Inner Hebrides with monastery founded by St. Columba; the centre of Celtic Christianity.
· *Adamnan* (l. 40): (c. 625–704 A.D.) abbot of the monastery at Iona and biographer of St. Columba.
❡ IN CAPERNAUM
· *Capernaum*: an ancient city of Palestine on the sea of Galilee.

Crawford, Isabella Valancy (1850–87) was born in Dublin, Ireland, and came to Canada with her family in 1858. Dr. Crawford's misappropriation of public funds led to a life of frequent dislocation and hardship for his family. In her later years, Crawford lived in poverty with her mother in Toronto prior to dying from heart failure. Although she wrote much prose, Crawford is especially remembered for her narrative poetry, some of which appeared in *Old Spookses' Pass, Malcolm's Katie, and Other Poems* (1884).

Creelman, David (b. 1962) was born in Nova Scotia. Having completed his M.A. at University of New Brunswick, he is now a doctoral student at York University.

Daniells, Roy (1902–79) was born in London, England, and came with his family to Victoria, B.C. in 1910. He was educated at U.B.C. and Toronto and taught English at Toronto, Manitoba, and U.B.C. His scholarly interests were in seventeenth-century English poetry, and he published two collections of poetry in his lifetime.

⁋ BROTHER LAWRENCE
   · *Bordeaux, Belfort* (ll. 8, 9): both major cities in France.
⁋ THE WICKET GATE
   · *Though lions roar* (l. 13): cf. Bunyan's popular hymn, "Who would true valour see" (from *The Pilgrim's Progress*).
⁋ BALLAD OF KINGSTON
   · *statue* (l. 3): of Sir John A. Macdonald.
   · *Apollonian* (l. 6): Apollo, Greek god portrayed in art as the perfection of youth and beauty.
   · *John A.* (l. 12): John A. Macdonald, first Canadian prime minister.
   · *Mazarin to Mackenzie King* (l. 17): Jules Mazarin (1602–61), French statesman. William Lyon Mackenzie King, prime minister of Canada in the 1920s and from 1935 to 1948.
   · *Zebedee* (l. 32): father of James and John.
⁋ ADESTE FIDELES
   · *title*: O come, all ye faithful.

Dempster, Barry (b. 1952) was born in Scarborough, Ont. He studied child psychology and currently works part-time at the Queen Street Mental Health Centre in Toronto. He has published a children's novel, a collection of short stories, and two books of poetry. A third collection is forthcoming: *Positions to Pray In* (Guernica Editions).

Dewart, Edward Hartley (1828–1903) was born in Ireland and came to Canada at six years of age. He was ordained a Methodist minister in 1855 and was editor of the *Christian Guardian* from 1869 until 1894. Dewart was the first anthologist of Canadian poetry (*Selections from Canadian Poets*, 1864) and published his own verse in *Songs of Life* (1869).

Ditsky, John (b. 1938) has been published in numerous poetry magazines in Canada and elsewhere. He teaches at the University of Windsor and is poetry editor of *University of Windsor Review*. He has published three collections of poetry in addition to three critical volumes and many critical articles and reviews.

⁋ SUCH LOVELY
   · *Daisy; Gatsbyed* (ll. 6–7): In *The Great Gatsby* (1925) by F. Scott Fitzgerald, Daisy is the ideal woman to whom Gatsby devotes his life. In one scene he displays all his shirts to her in a pathetic attempt to win her approval of his wealth and status.
   · *hieratic* (l. 12): priestly (synonymn of sacerdotal).

Finch, Robert (b. 1900) was born of English parents in New York, and eventually taught French for forty years at the University of Toronto. He is also an accomplished painter and musician. He has published scholarly work in addition to many volumes of poetry, two of which received Governor-General's Awards (*Poems* in 1946 and *Acis in Oxford* in 1961.) His most recent volume is *For the Back of a Likeness* (1986).

℘ NOWELL, NOWELL
- *clout* (l. 17): cloth.
- *shindy* (l. 24): disturbance.
- *pip* (l. 25): spot on playing cards, dice, or dominoes; hence game.

℘ THE ANSWER
- *The past is prologue* (l. 7): *The Tempest*, Act II, sc.i, l. 253.
- *Buchenwald* (l. 15): site of Nazi concentration camp.
- *Iago* (l. 16): villain of Shakespeare's *Othello*.
- *fain* (l. 60): glad to.

℘ THE ROOM
- *unprocrustean* (l. 3): Prokroustes, a robber who fitted victims to his bed by stretching or mutilation.
- *Gamaliel* (l. 12): a doctor of the law (a Pharisee) who taught Saul of Tarsus (Acts 22:3).

℘ THE EXEGETE
- *sea of faith* (l. 1): cf. Matthew Arnold, "Dover Beach."

Fox, Gail (b. 1942) was born in Willimantic, Connecticut, and later studied at Cornell before coming to Canada. She now lives with her husband, Fred Cogswell, in New Brunswick. She has published several volumes of poetry, the most recent of which is *The Deepening of the Colours* (Oberon, 1986).

℘ THOMAS MERTON
- *title*: Merton (1915–69) was a Roman Catholic monk well-known as an author and poet.

Gibbon, Timothy (b. 1940) was born in Pennsylvania and grew up in Philadelphia. She later studied at McGill and lived for several years in Toronto. She and her family now live on Saltspring Island, B.C.

℘ EL TESTIGO
- *title*: the witness.
- *epigraph*: "Lord, you have opened my eyes; / Smiling, you have called my name. / On the beach I have left my boat. / Together with you, I will sail another sea."
- *Kabbalists* (l. 19): cabalist; adherent to occult religious philosophy developed by certain Jewish rabbis and based on a mystical interpretation of Scripture.
- *conquistadores* (l. 20): Spanish conquerors in Mexico, Peru, etc.
- *Ola!* (l. 30): Hullo!
- *Ciao!* (l. 37): good bye or so long.

· *con cuidado* (l. 43): with care.
❡ DRINA JOUBERT 1914–85
  · *title*: Joubert was a Toronto "bag lady" who was found frozen to death in the cab of a truck.
  · *Sistering* (l. 5): Toronto organization helping women.

Gibbs, Robert (b. 1930) was born in Saint John, N.B. He was educated at U.N.B. and Cambridge (Ph.D., 1970) and is now Professor of English at U.N.B. Since 1968 he has edited, or helped edit, *The Fiddlehead* magazine. The most recent of his six collections is *The Tongue Still Dances*.

Hayes, Glenn (b. 1948) was born in Sarnia, Ont. He currently lives in Newmarket, Ont., and teaches school in Schomberg. He has published in various magazines and journals and is preparing his first collection, *Roadsongs for the Walking Third*, for publication.

❡ IN REVERSE
  · *Salonika* (l. 1): seaport in Macedonia, Greece.
❡ DENIALS
  · *Where I go* . . . . (l. 16): cf. John 13:36.
  · *Wait a little while* . . . . (l. 18): cf. John 16: 16–17.
  · *Cock crew* (l. 35): cf. Mark 14: 68, 72.

Helwig, Maggie (b. 1961) was born in Liverpool, England, and now lives in Toronto. She has published several collections of poetry, the most recent being *Eden* from Oberon Press. "A Second Procession" is from *A Mass For The Life Of The World*, co-authored with Tim Lilburn.

❡ A SECOND PROCESSION
  · *Arles* (l. 29): city in southern France.
  · *Turner* (l. 31): J.M.W. Turner (1775–1851), English painter.
  · *El Salvador* (l. 33): Central American country.
  · *slip, slide* (l. 37): cf. T.S. Eliot, *Burnt Norton*, section v (*The Four Quartets*).
❡ THE CONVERSION OF ST. PAUL
  · *epigraph*: cf. Acts 9.
  · *Ananias* (l. 22): cf. Acts 9: 10–18.
❡ THE SECRETS OF ENOCH
  · *Uruk* (l. 10): ancient Sumerian city on the Euphrates in Babylonia.

Herbert, Mary (1829–72) was born in Halifax and, with her sister Sarah, raised in a strict environment of Methodism and temperance. She published occasional verse, founded a women's periodical (*The Mayflower*), and also wrote novellas, prose sketches, and didactic novels. She published two volumes of verse in her lifetime.

❡ STANZAS
  · *epigraph*: 1 Samuel 3: 9, 10.

- *voice* (l. 10): 1 Kings 19:12
- *land* (l. 17): cf. Hebrews 11:16

Johnson, Pauline (1861–1913) was born near Brantford, Canada West (Ontario), on the Six Nations Reserve. She was the daughter of an English mother (Emily Howells) and a Mohawk father. After her appearance in W. D. Lighthall's anthology, *Songs of the Great Dominion* (1889), Johnson became well known for her entertaining public readings, sometimes in full Indian dress. She retired to Vancouver in 1909.

¶ A PRODIGAL
- *rue* (l. 3): remorse.

Johnston, George (b. 1913) was born in Hamilton, Ont. After time as a freelance writer in England and service with the RCAF in World War II, he took graduate studies at the University of Toronto. He taught Anglo-Saxon and Old Norse for thirty years at Carleton University and has published several collections of poetry.

¶ DAISIES
- *fiat mihi* (l. 5): be it unto me.

Kennedy, Leo (b. 1907) was born in Liverpool, England, and moved with his family to Montreal in 1912. He studied business at the Université de Montréal and met A. J. M. Smith and F. R. Scott, other writers interested in modernist poetics. He published one collection, *The Shrouding* (1933), and his poems were included in the avant-garde anthology, *New Provinces* (1936).

¶ SOLILOQUY FOR BELLS
- *Angelus* (l. 9): devotional exercise commemorating Incarnation and said at the sounding of a bell.
- *Vespers* (l. 10): principal evening office in the Christian Church.
- *Matins* (l. 11): properly a midnight office but also recited at daybreak; morning prayer in the Church of England.

Kirkconnell, Watson (1895–1977) was born in Port Hope, Ont., and educated at Queen's, Toronto Conservatory of Music, and Oxford. He had a long and distinguished academic career at Wesley College (Winnipeg), McMaster, and Acadia University. An immensely prolific scholar, Kirkconnell did translations of poetry from over fifty languages, helped found the Canadian Authors' Association, and worked to create the Humanities Research Council. He published many collections of poetry during his lifetime.

Lampman, Archibald (1861–99) was born in Morpeth, Canada West (Ontario), the son of an Anglican clergyman. He attended Trinity College, Toronto, and after an unsuccessful stint of teaching he became a clerk in the Post Office Department, Ottawa. Duncan Campbell Scott, another government employee, became a friend with whom Lampman took canoe trips. After Lampman's early death, Scott did much to promote his friend's reputation as a poet. Lampman is now considered the finest of the Confederation poets, especially notable for his nature poetry.

Lane, M. Travis (b. 1934) was born in the U.S. and studied at Vassar (B.A.) and Cornell (Ph.D). She is now an Honorary Research Associate, Department of English, U.N.B. She has written critical essays and review articles on contemporary poetry and is the author of several books of poetry, including the Pat Lowther prize winner *Divinations, and Shorter Poems 1973–1978. Reckonings*, her fifth book, is forthcoming from Fiddlehead Poetry Books (1988).

❡ THE BANDERLOG
  · *title*: Author's note: "The Banderlog and Baloo and Bagheera [l. 9] are all references to the *Just So Stories* by Rudyard Kipling in which a little boy, Mowgli, is adopted by a tribe of wolves. His wolf parents ask two teachers of great wisdom to instruct the child in the Law of the Jungle and in its various languages (how to ask help from a kite or a snake, for example). Baloo is the wise bear, an individual; Bagheera the wise panther, again an individual. The Banderlog (which Kipling capitalizes) is the tribe of monkeys, who are regarded with contempt by the rest of the jungle, for they have no law, no dignity, no honour. Thus, in the third line of the poem, 'God's monkey-thought' 'is us,' the anthropoids."
❡ WELL, VIEWED BY GOD
  · *Dis* (l. 11): Roman god of the lower world.
  · *Pandora* (l. 17): in Greek mythology, the first mortal woman who, in opening a box given to her by Zeus, released all human ills into the world.
  · *fey* (l. 21): unusually excited.
  · *Bluebeard's wife* (l. 23): Bluebeard is a character in an old story who married, and then murdered, several wives.
  · *that cost her . . . .* (l. 38): Milton, *Paradise Lost* 4.271.

Leprohon, Mrs. Rosanna (1829–79) was born in Montreal and began publishing in *The Literary Garland* in 1846 under the initials R.E.M. and later Rosanna Mullins. Her marriage to Jean-Lucien Leprohon produced thirteen children. She wrote several novels, and her poetry was collected by John Lovell after her death (*The Poetical Works of Mrs. Leprohon*, 1881).

Leslie, Kenneth (1892–1974) was born in Nova Scotia. He was educated at Dalhousie (B.A. 1914) and at U. of Nebraska. Among his several books of poetry, *By Stubborn Stars* won the Governor-General's Award for poetry in 1938. That same year Leslie founded the *Protestant Digest*, a journal that espoused his socialist and Christian humanist ideas. Dissatisfied with a selection of his poetry published in 1970 by Ladysmith Press in Quebec, Leslie published his own selected verse in 1971, *O'Malley to the Reds*.

¶ GOD'S ANSWER TO A PSALMIST
· *title*: cf. Psalm 8:4.

Lilburn, Tim (b. 1950) was born in Regina, Saskatchewan. He now lives in Kitchener, Ont., and does some teaching and volunteer work with the unemployed. He has published in several magazines and his first collection, *Names of God*, was published by Oolichan Press in 1986. "Call to Worship" and "Celebrant's Greeting" are from *A Mass For The Life Of The World*, co-authored with Maggie Helwig.

¶ CALL TO WORSHIP IN A MASS FOR THE LIFE OF THE WORLD
· *Vespucci* (l. 23): Amerigo Vespucci (1451–1512), Italian navigator after whom America is named.
· *pax* (l. 25): peace.
· *Nathaniel* (l. 26): one of the first disciples of Jesus who recommended him for his sincerity.
· *Alden* (l. 28): Alden Nowlan (1933–83), Canadian poet.
· *William* (l. 34): William Kurelek (1927–77), Canadian painter, writer, evangelist.
¶ CELEBRANT'S GREETING
· *O taste and see* (l. 14): a phrase used in modern liturgies of the Eucharist (see Psalm 34:8).
¶ SERMON TO A BARN OF DAIRY GOATS AT PENTECOST
· *Hegel* (l. 7): G.W.F. Hegel (1770–1831), German philosopher.
· *Duns Scotus* (l. 7): (1265?–1308?), Scottish theologian.
· *Isadora Duncan* (l. 14): (1878–1927), American dancer.
· *yurodivetsvo* (l. 22): Russian for "fools of Christ."
· *Victor Mature* (l. 23): Hollywood star of 1950s.

Lochhead, Douglas (b. 1922) was born in Guelph, Ont. He was educated at McGill and Toronto and has been on the library staffs of Victoria College, Cornell, Dalhousie, York, and Toronto universities. In recent years he has been Professor of Canadian Studies at Mount Allison University. He is now writer-in-residence at Mt. Allison. His new and selected poems were published in *Tiger in the Skull* (1986).

¶ AT THE TOP
· *boreal* (l. 20): northern.
¶ DEAD GULL
· *combers* (l. 5): breaker or long curling wave.

MacDonald, J. E. H. (1873–1932) was born in England. He trained as a painter in Hamilton and Toronto and later was a founding member of the Group of Seven. He wrote poetry in the latter part of his life.

Mackay, Louis (1901–83) was born in Hensall, Ontario, and educated at the University of Toronto and Oxford. Later a professor of classics at Toronto, British Columbia, and California, he first used the pseudonym "John Smalacombe" in publishing his poems (*Viper's Bugloss*, 1938). He later published *The Ill-Tempered Lover and Other Poems* (1948) under his own name.

❡ REND YOUR HEARTS . . . .
· *paladins* (l. 8): a knight or champion.
❡ CAROL FOR 1938
· *Barcelona, Chungking* (ll. 5, 6): Spanish and Chinese cities where military battles had recently involved civilian casualties.
· *tryst* (l. 14): rendezvous, appointment.

Macpherson, Jay (b. 1931) was born in England and came to Canada at age nine. She was educated at Carleton, McGill, and University of Toronto (M.A., 1955; Ph.D., 1964) and now teaches English at Victoria College. Her first commercially published book, *The Boatman* (1957), won a Governor-General's Award for poetry.

❡ THE FISHERMAN
· hoicks (l. 24): to force to turn abruptly upwards.

MacSween, R.J. (b. 1915) was born in Glace Bay, N.S. After graduating from St. Francis Xavier University, he became a priest and did parish work for several years. He returned to St. Francis Xavier and taught English there from 1948 to 1985. He was co-founder of the *Antigonish Review* and was its editor for ten years. He has published four books of poetry, a collection of short stories, and a novel.

❡ THE HERETICS
· *Berengarius* (l. 33): Berengar of Tours (c. 1000–1088?), French theologian who disagreed with established views of the Eucharist. Though declared a heretic, he was reconciled with the church before he died and the controversy led to a more explicit formulation of the doctrine of the Eucharist.

McLachlan, Alexander (1818–96) emigrated to Canada from Scotland in 1840 to assume the farm of his deceased father. He later worked as a tailor and an immigration agent. McLachlan published five volumes of poetry and became known for both his pioneer poetry and his strong democratic sentiments.

❡ OLD HANNAH
· *burn* (l. 10): little stream.
· *wimpling*: meandering.
· *peace* (l. 32): see Philippians 4:7.

McCaslin, Susan (b. 1947) was born in Indianapolis, Indiana and educated at the University of Washington (B.A. 1969), Simon Fraser (M.A. 1973), and University of British Columbia (Ph.D. 1984). She currently teaches at Douglas College in New Westminister, B.C. She has appeared in numerous literary periodicals in Canada and elsewhere and has published five volumes of poetry, the most recent being *Conversing with Paradise* (Vancouver: Golden Eagle Press, 1986)

¶ JOHN OF THE CROSS II (Cautery)
· *Cautery*: an instrument or substance for cauterizing (burning tissue to prevent the spread of infection).

McGee, Thomas D'Arcy (1825–68) was born in Ireland and immigrated to Boston in 1842 where he worked as a journalist. He moved to Montreal in 1857 and soon became more directly involved in politics on behalf of the disadvantaged Irish; he was elected to the Legislative Assembly of the Province of Canada in 1858. McGee was assassinated in 1868 by a Fenian because of his support for Confederation. In addition to his writings about Ireland and Canada, he published one volume of verse (1858); his poetry was collected after his death in *The Poems of Thomas D'Arcy McGee* (New York, 1869).

¶ THE THREE SISTERS
· *sisters* (l. 1): see 1 Corinthians 13, especially verse 13.
· *Laves* (l. 8): wash.
· *anchor* (l. 9): traditional emblem of hope.

McPherson, John (1817–45) was born in Nova Scotia. Unable to support himself simply by poetry, he became a schoolteacher in 1841, married, and had a daughter. His frail health soon deteriorated, however, and he died in July 1845. His poems were posthumously collected and edited by John S. Thompson in *Poems, Descriptive and Moral by John McPherson* (1862).

¶ PROBATION
· *to redeem* . . . . (l. 1): cf. Ephesians 5:16.

Moodie, Susanna (1803–85) was born in England but, after her marriage to John Moodie, immigrated to Canada in 1832 where she continued to write stories, novels, and poems. "Paraphrase" is from *Enthusiasm, and Other Poems* (1831). She is best known for the autobiographical *Roughing It in the Bush: Or, Life in Canada* (1852).

¶ PARAPHRASE: PSALM XLIV
· *terrific* (l. 15): terrifying.

Outram, Richard (b. 1930) was born in Oshawa. He studied at Victoria College, University of Toronto, and has worked for the Canadian Broadcasting Corporation for many years. His several collections of poetry have sometimes included visual art done by his wife, artist Barbara Howard. His selected poems were published in 1984 by Exile Editions. *Hiram and Jenny* is his newest collection (Porcupine's Quill, 1988).

❡ VOCATIONS
  · *the merveiles by thy mercie wrought* (l. 21): from Spenser's "Hymn of Heavenly Love," l. 49.
  · *Milton's echo*: possibly *Paradise Lost* 1.21.
❡ OTHER
  · *Misprisioned* (l. 8): concealed.

Parr, Michael (b. 1927) was born in London, England, and immigrated to Canada in the post-war years. He published *The Green Fig Tree* with Macmillan in 1965, and his work has appeared in many periodicals as well as in anthologies. He works in the printing industry in Toronto.

Pickthall, Marjorie (1883–1922) was born in England and came to Canada as a child. Though she worked for a time in the library at Victoria College and during the war as a farm labourer, her health was always precarious. She moved to Vancouver in 1920 but died there of an embolus. Besides the two collections of poetry for which she is best known, she also published short stories and novels.

❡ PÈRE LALEMENT
  · *title*: Gabriel Lalemant was one of five Jesuit fathers killed by the Iroquois Indians near Ste. Marie Among The Hurons.
  · *byre* (l. 8): cow barn.
  · *Mont Royal, Stadacona* (l. 22): early names for Montreal and Quebec City.
  · *St. Ignace, St. Louis* (l. 27, l. 29): missionary outposts built by the Jesuits in seventeenth-century Canada.
  · *Hiram, Sidonian cedars* (ll. 32–33): Hiram, King of Tyre (979–945 B.C.), friend of David and Solomon; Sidon was the ancient seaport of the Phoenicians.
  · *scrip* (l. 39): pilgrim's wallet or satchel.
❡ SALUTARIS HOSTIA
  · *title:* O saving victim.
  · *lucent* (l. 12): shining, luminous.
  · *Sharon's Rose* (l. 23): Sharon is a plain on the coast of Israel. The epithet describes Christ.
❡ DEUS MISEREATUR:
  · *title*: God so loved.

Pratt, E.J. (1882–1964) was born in Newfoundland. After graduating from St. John's Methodist College, he preached and taught in outlying communities before coming to Toronto to attend Victoria College. Three years after receiving a Ph.D. in theology (1917), he joined Victoria's English

Department and taught there for over thirty years. Pratt's reputation is based largely on his narrative poems, and he received three Governor-General's Awards for poetry in his lifetime.

¶ THE DEPRESSION ENDS
- *Prospero* (1. 2): magician in Shakespeare's *The Tempest.*
- *dinner* (1. 12): cf. Luke 14:12–24.
- *gruel* (1. 28): broth.
- *Tishbite* (1. 49): 1 Kings 17:1–6.
- *Orion, Taurus, Centaurus* (ll. 53–55): names of constellations.
- *Wain* (1. 57): Charles's Wain; seven bright stars in the Big Dipper.
- *Pleiades* (1. 62): stars in constellation Taurus.
- *Lepus* (1. 63): constellation.
- *Monoceros* (1. 66): The Unicorn.
- *terrapin* (1. 67): turtle.
- *Hesperides* (1. 72): in Greek mythology, the garden where the golden apples grew.
- *Gemini, Castor, Pollux* (ll. 179–81): the constellation Gemini contains the stars Castor and Pollux.
- *Capricornis* (1. 83): southern constellation.
- *Canis Major* (1. 84): another southern constellation with Sirius its brightest star.
- *Aquarius* (1. 86): constellation.
- *Neptune* (1. 87): god of the sea.
- *Cetus* (1. 88): constellation.
- *Argo* (1. 90): constellation.
- *Alpha . . . .* (1. 101): opening letters of the Greek alphabet.
- *Auriga, Capella* (1. 106, 1. 108): a northern constellation and its brightest star.
- *spigots* (1. 113): plug in a barrel.
- *ambrosial* (1. 115): ambrosia, food for the gods.
- *obsequies* (1. 120): funeral rite.
- *purees* (1. 121): thick soup.
- *Spica, ragout* (1. 122): bright star in constellation Virgo; highly seasoned stew.
- *Cygnus, Aries* (ll. 124–25): constellations.
- *syllabubs* (1. 138): a frothy dessert or beverage of cream, wine, and cider.
- *prognathic* (1. 146): abnormally projecting jaw.
- *seven years* (1. 191): cf. Genesis 41:9–36.
- *salubrious* (1. 217): healthful.
- *Aurora, Portico* (1. 226): goddess of dawn; the Painted Porch at Athens.

Reade, John (1837–1919) was born and educated in Ireland and came to Canada in 1856. He studied both law and theology (he was ordained in 1864) but became literary editor of the *Montreal Gazette* in 1870, a position he held for the rest of his life. He was a charter member of the Royal

Society of Canada (1882) and published *The Prophecy of Merlin, and Other Poems* in 1870.

Reibetanz, John (b. 1944) was born in New York City and educated at S.U.N.Y. and Princeton. He now teaches English at the University of Toronto. Besides a study of *King Lear* (1977), he has published one collection of poetry, *Ashbourn* (Véhicule Press, 1986).

¶ GREAT HOUSE, SOUTH AFRICA
· *bons mots* (l. 5): witticisms.
¶ ANDREW WHITTAKER, LOCAL PREACHER
· *my text, "the grass . . . . "* (l. 20): 2 Kings 19:26.
· *dibbling* (l. 23): a dibble is a pointed tool used to make holes in the soil for seeds, bulbs, or young plants.
· *our Lord's "much"* (l. 25): cf. Matthew 6:30.
· *green in the morning* (l. 27): cf. Psalm 119:147.

Roberts, Sir Charles G.D. (1860–1943) was born in Douglas, N.B., educated at the University of New Brunswick, and taught in Nova Scotia for ten years before moving to New York, London, and then the continent. He returned to Canada in 1925 and lived in Toronto for the remainder of his life. Roberts has been called the "father" of Canadian literature because of the acclamation his early poetry received internationally. Besides being the author of numerous volumes of poetry, he was also a prolific prose writer and has been described as the inventor of the modern animal story.

¶ A CHILD'S PRAYER AT EVENING
· *Domine . . . .* (epigraph): O Lord, who keepest the stars in thy care.
¶ BEYOND THE TOPS OF TIME
· *lambent* (l. 22): softly radiant.
· *sard, chrysoprase* (l. 31): precious stones, both varieties of quartz, the first orange and the second green. For ll. 31–36, cf. Revelation 21:10 ff.
¶ ASCRIPTION
· *speedwell* (l. 7): a flower.
· *Arcturus* (l. 12): brightest star in the constellation Boötes.
¶ TO A CERTAIN MYSTIC
· *shallop* (l. 6): dinghy.
· *Elysian* (l. 7): paradise in Greek mythology.

Ross, W. W. E. (1894–1966) was born in Peterborough, Ont., and worked all his life as a geophysicist at the Dominion Magnetic Observatory in Agincourt, Ont. He published infrequently, but he has become recognized as Canada's first Imagist poet.

¶ ON ANGELS
· *circumambient* (l. 7): surrounding.

Sangster, Charles (1822–93) was born in Kingston, Upper Canada. He spent much of his life working as a journalist but latterly was employed by the federal post office. He published three collections of verse and became known as the poet laureate of colonial Canada.

❡ MY PRAYER
- *voice* (l. 11): cf. 1 Kings 19:12.
- *Peace . . .* (l. 12): Mark 4:39.
- *Rock* (l. 32): Matthew 16:18.

Scott, Duncan Campbell (1862–1947) was born in Ottawa and worked as a civil servant in the Department of Indian Affairs (then known as the Indian Branch). Many of his poems sympathize with the plight of native people. In addition to several volumes of poetry, Scott wrote short stories, a play, two biographies, and edited poems by Lampman (whose literary executor he became).

❡ MEDITATION AT PERUGIA
- *Perugia*: city in central Italy.
- *Umbrian* (l. 2): region in central Italy.
- *Trevi, Spello* (ll. 3–4): towns in central Italy.
- *Assisi* (l. 7): birthplace of St. Francis.

Scott, F. G. (1861–1944) was born in Montreal and educated at Bishop's College in Lennoxville, Quebec. He was ordained priest in Essex, England, in 1886 and eventually returned to Canada where he soon became rector of St. Matthew's Church in Quebec City. He was senior chaplain to the Canadian First Division during World War I and his courageous behaviour at the front became well known. He wrote poetry that expressed his patriotism, religious convictions, and feelings about the natural world.

❡ THE SNOWSTORM
- *Triune* (l. 9): three in one.

❡ IN TE, DOMINE
- *title*: In Thee, O Lord.

❡ REQUIESCANT
- *title*: let them rest.

Scott, F. R. (1899–1985) was born in Quebec City, the sixth of seven children of Amy and F.G. Scott. He taught law for most of his career at McGill but was also very active in the Canadian socialist movement. In addition to essays on constitutional law and translations of French Canadian poetry, he published several volumes of poetry and his *Collected Poems* (1981) won the Governor-General's Award for poetry.

Smith, A. J. M. (1902–80) was born in Montreal and educated at McGill and Edinburgh (Ph.D., 1931). Finding no positions available in Canada, he taught at various American colleges until he was appointed at Michigan

State College. Smith is one of the most important figures in twentieth-century Canadian poetry because of his vigorous promotion of modernism and disciplined writing, through his own literary criticism, his poetry (five collections), and his editing of anthologies.

Smith, Kay (b. 1911) was born in Saint John, New Brunswick. After graduating from Mount Allison University, she taught in St. Thomas, Ont., and in Saint John. In recent years she has taught creative writing at the University of New Brunswick. In addition to being published in anthologies and literary magazines, she has published four collections of poetry, the most recent being *The Bright Particulars* (Ragweed Press, 1987).

Swiss, Margo (b. 1946) was born in Peterborough, Ont. She was educated at Trent, Manitoba, and York (Ph. D., 1981) where she has been teaching for several years. Her poetry has appeared in magazines and in an anthology edited by Gary Geddes (*The Inner Ear*, 1983).

❡ I THIRST
· *title*: cf. John 19:28, and also George Herbert, "The Agonie": "Love is that liquor sweet and most divine, / Which my God feels as bloud; but I, as wine."

Thibaudeau, Colleen (b. 1925) was born in Toronto but grew up in St. Thomas, Ont. She attended the University of Toronto (B.A., 1948; M.A., 1949) and in 1951 married James Reaney. She has lived in London, Ont., since 1960. She has appeared in several anthologies and has published three books of poetry, the most recent of which is *The Martha Landscapes* (Brick Books, 1984).

❡ THE BROWN FAMILY
· *Caen* (l. 14): in Normandy, France, where Allies invaded occupied France during World War II.
· *Teazle* (l. 25): teasel; Fuller's teasel is a thistle-like plant.
· *suvendibly* (l. 28): completely.
· *Anna Pauker* (l. 29): Communist guerilla in Eastern Europe.
❡ FROM "THE PLANNED WOODLOT TO THE FREEDOM OF MRS. FIELD"
· *Glendalough* (l. 3): here and below, the place names refer to Ireland.
· *Claudine* (l. 17): Sidonie G. Colette (1873–1954) collaborated with her first husband Willy on the five novels of the Claudine series (1900–07).
· *big Grayling*: a fish of the trout family.

Watson, Wilfred (b. 1911) was born in England and immigrated with his family to B.C. in 1926. After several years of sawmill work, he studied at U.B.C. and, after the war, at Toronto (Ph.D., 1951). He taught subsequently at the University of Alberta with his wife Sheila Watson. Watson's later poetry is highly experimental, as is his drama. His first collection, *Friday's*

Child (1955), won a Governor-General's Award for poetry.

¶ CANTICLE OF DARKNESS
· *Canticle*: song or hymn.

Whalley, George (1915–83) was born in Kingston, Ont. He was educated at Bishop's and Oxford (prior to extensive service during World War II) and at London (Ph.D., 1950) afterwards. In a distinguished academic career he taught at Queen's University for thirty years and was internationally recognized as a Coleridge scholar. In addition to numerous scholarly publications, he published two collections of poetry. His *Collected Poems* was recently edited by George Johnston (Quarry Press, 1986).

¶ LAZARUS
· *bladderwrack* (l. 10): common seaweed.
· *lapis lazuli* (l. 17): a gem, deep blue, violet, or greenish blue and often flecked with yellow iron pyrites.
· *fricture of cicadas* (l. 29): fricture seems to be a neologism. Cicadas are large insects with transparent wings; the male makes a loud, shrill sound by vibrating a special sound organ on its undersurface.
· *spikenard* (l. 57): fragrant oil or ointment made from a herb.

Wreford, James (b. 1915; pseudonym for James Wreford Watson) was born in Scotland and was educated at the University of Edinburgh. He began the Department of Geography at McMaster University in 1938 and in 1949 became Chief Geographer, Canada. In 1955 he returned to Edinburgh to start a Programme of North American Studies, from which the Centre of Canadian Studies (which he headed in 1972) originated. He has appeared in numerous anthologies of Canadian poetry and his collection *Of Time and the Lover* won the Governor-General's Award for poetry (1950).

¶ THE ANGEL IN THE WOOD
· *geodesy* (l. 7): a branch of mathematics dealing with the size and shape of the earth.

Yule, Mrs. J.C. (1825–1897) was born in New York and educated in Michigan. She was appointed an instructor in English art and literature at the Canadian Literary Institute in Woodstock, Ont., in 1860. Her *Poems of the Heart and Home* was published in 1881.